Strategic Planning in Higher Education

Implementing New Roles for the Academic Library

Strategic Planning in Higher Education

Implementing New Roles for the Academic Library

76632

James F. Williams, II
Editor

The Haworth Press
New York • London

Strategic Planning in Higher Education: Implementing New Roles for the Academic Library has also been published as *Journal of Library Administration*, Volume 13, Numbers 3/4.

The Haworth Press, Inc. 10 Alice Street, Binghamton, NY 13904-1580
EUROSPAN/Haworth, 3 Henrietta Street, London WC2E 8LU England

Library of Congress Cataloging-in-Publication Data

Strategic planning in higher education : implementing new roles for the academic library / James F. Williams II, editor.
    p. cm.
   "Has also been published as Journal of library administration, volume 13, numbers 3/4, 1990" — T.p. verso.
    ISBN 1-56024-091-1 (alk. paper)
   1. Libraries, University and college — United States — Administration. 2. Strategic planning — United States. 3. Library planning — United States.
Z675.U5S82 1991
027.7'0973 — dc20

                                90-26627
                                  CIP

Strategic Planning in Higher Education
Implementing New Roles
for the Academic Library

CONTENTS

Introduction   1
>   E. Gordon Gee
>   James F. Williams, II

Strategic Planning and Management: A Methodology
for Responsible Change   9
>   James M. Rosser
>   James I. Penrod

Strategic Planning at Iowa State University: Affirmation
and Expectations   35
>   Gordon P. Eaton
>   Jean W. Adams

Inserting the Library into a Broader Campus Planning
Process   53
>   Nancy L. Eaton

The Dreams of the Reasonable: Integrating Library
and University Planning   63
>   Jinnie Y. Davis
>   Karen P. Helm

Refocusing, Rebalancing, and Refining(R³): The Libraries'
Role in Strategic Long-Range Planning
at Michigan State University   79
>   Beth J. Shapiro

The University of Iowa Libraries' Strategic Plan   99
>   Barbara I. Dewey

The Library Long-Range Planning Process at Wayne State   113
    Eileen M. Mulhare

Transforming the Library: Strategic Planning at Bradley
  University — The University Perspective   131
    Martin G. Abegg
    Kalman Goldberg

Transforming the Library: Strategic Planning at Bradley
  University — The Library Perspective   137
    Ellen I. Watson

Conformity and Diversity: Local Library Planning
in a Multi-Campus System   147
    Russell Shank

Planning for Diversity: Strategic Planning for an Urban
  Academic Library   157
    Marilyn Mitchell
    Rutherford W. Witthus

University Libraries and Academic Strategic Planning
at the University of Cincinnati   167
    Linda J. Cain
    William F. Louden

A Strategic Planning Process for the Multi-Campus
University System: The Role of One Campus
and Its Library   181
    Leslie A. Manning

A Strategic Planning Imperative: The Penn State Experience   201
    Nancy M. Cline
    Salvatore M. Meringolo

ABOUT THE EDITOR

James Williams, II, MSLS, is the Dean of Libraries at the University of Colorado at Boulder. He holds a library degree from Atlanta University and is a Visiting Scholar and Senior Fellow at the UCLA Graduate School of Library and Information Science. Mr. Williams has served on the Board of Regents of the National Library of Medicine, and he is currently a member of the ARL Task Force on Telecommunications, and the Research Libraries Advisory Committee to OCLC. His professional interests include academic library administration, national research and education networking, and leadership for research libraries.

Introduction

American institutions of higher education have been so busy managing the assaults of McCarthyism and then the upheavals of Civil Rights, the Vietnam War, and the youth movement, so busy coping with demographic decline, a savage inflation, and the multiple demands of multiple constituencies, including vast changes in internal governance and the need to run the business parts of themselves like businesses, that they have not since the end of World War II and the Korean War redefined themselves. . . . American institutions in general and those for higher education in particular have been coping, but they have not adapted to changing times, and they are no longer perceived as leading. They are not perceived as leading, because, in fact, the institutions themselves while being competently managed in most cases, are not necessarily themselves being led. Management is the capacity to handle multiple problems, neutralize various constituencies, motivate personnel; in a college or university, it means hitting as well the actual budget at break-even. Leadership, on the other hand, is an essentially moral act. It is the assertion of a vision, not simply the exercise of a style; the moral courage to assert a vision of the institution in the future and the intellectual energy to persuade the community or the culture of the wisdom and validity of the vision. It is to make the vision practicable, and compelling.[1]

A. Bartlett Giamatti

This volume is devoted to the process of vision-setting and the establishment of academic strategy which has come to be commonplace in higher education after some 22 years of experimentation. The articles have been authored by college and university presidents, campus planners, and librarians. And, the focus is on the plannning process and its ultimate meaning to the academy and its library.

The literature of management defines strategic planning as any planning activity concerned with the long-term future in broad outline, with summaries of objectives, resources to be used, and methods.[2] While still crude, the processes being applied in higher education today have at least matured to the point where we know what not to do when bringing planning and organizational politics together to formulate and implement academic strategy. According to Keller, it is important to understand that strategic planning is not (i) the construction of a blueprint, (ii) a set of platitudes, (iii) the personal vision of the president or board of trustees, (iv) a collection of departmental plans, compiled and edited, (v) a process done by planners, (vi) a substitution of numbers for important intangibles, (vii) a form of surrender to market conditions and trends, (viii) something done on an annual retreat, (ix) a way of eliminating risks, and (x) an attempt to read tea leaves and outwit the future.[3] To the contrary, academic strategy setting has come to be viewed as a useful management tool in an environment where the educational process is complex, where change is large and constant, and where uncertainty is high. It has come to be used as an effective means to manage change, with a focus on resource allocation and an emphasis on investing in strategies. Its process is analytical and qualitative, and if done well, it results in strategic decisions on timing, priority and context, driven by the vision of the institution. Taken further, it pulls together a diverse educational enterprise, communicates a clear set of strategic objectives and institutional values, and achieves the creative integration of institutional resources.

Libraries in academia today must assume an ever increasing central and integral role in the establishment of institutional policy on information access and use. This can only be accomplished as a collaborative effort between librarians, administrators, and the creators of the scholarly record. A recent award-winning article on the model library states that boundary conditions and transitional steps will alter research libraries radically by the year 2020. Functions, organization, administration, staffing, results, and the library's centrality on campus will be altered, with service clusters formed and disbanded to meet the needs of client groups. Flexibility, collaboration, diversity, and fluidity will characterize research library operation and service.[4] The authors in this collection share this bold vision in a series of articles which describe their efforts to devise plans which define what should exist in order to achieve a library organization of dimension and quality appropriate to that vision.

The highlight of this volume is its joint message from college and university presidents, campus planners, and librarians on planning as a campus activity. Readers will find the following common themes running through these articles:

1. The intended product of planning is communication, and not a formal document;
2. The planning exercise helps the members of the academic community understand how institutional decisions are made, and how to become more competitive for limited institutional resources;
3. With refreshing candor, it is acknowledged that the incentive for strategic planning stems from unfavorable circumstances, whether rapid economic decline and hardship, declining enrollments, the suggestion that some academic programs were no longer appropriate, or the increasing constraints of public and private funding that have become serious factors for institutions of higher education throughout the nation; and
4. The integration of library planning in the college and university-wide planning process gives the library's goals more prominence among campus administrators.

Whatever the reasons for initiating planning, readers will find the general approaches to the process remarkably similar as described here, but with varying degrees of participation by faculty, librarians, and administration. A brief summary and highlights of the papers in their order of presentation follows.

President James Rosser of California State University, Los Angeles, and his Vice President for Information Resources Management, James Penrod, provide a description of the rationale behind an urban university's decision to adopt a formal planning process. This article includes a description of the Shirley planning model and other instruments used in the planning process. The authors go so far as to cite George Keller's dictum that the catalysts for change in higher education come from one of three sources: a major crisis, the exertion of pressure from the outside, or a vigorous, farsighted leader. In paraphrase, these catalysts are then described as crisis, lust, or good fortune, and CSLA acknowledges that all three contributed to its decision to begin strategic planning. Librarians will be interested in the authors' views on libraries as supply-oriented vs. demand-driven organizations; likewise, their thoughts on libraries and the emerging National Research and Education Network.

President Gordon Eaton of Iowa State University and his Associate Provost, Jean Adams, discuss a planning activity with specific emphasis on Iowa State's heritage as the nation's first land-grant institution. The paper is highlighted by President Eaton's charge to the planning committee to think "unthinkable" thoughts and speak "unspeakable" words during its deliberations to create a sharper institutional focus. It is noted that the President specifically sought a planning committee of "statesman-like individuals who would be willing to take part in protracted rational discussions of the possible elimination of their own academic units." Readers should give attention to the well-defined review process that took place at Iowa State, and the authors' advice on institutional self-examination.

Nancy Eaton is the new Dean of Library Services at Iowa State University and her paper describes the process of meshing a campus planning process already underway with a new internal planning process for the libraries; this, in the face of serious internal institutional circumstances and external state-planning circumstances. The highlight of this paper is its tie to the previous paper and the strategy and decisions made by the library administration in this fascinating case study.

Jinnie Davis is the planning officer for the libraries at North Carolina State University and Karen Helm is the University's planning officer. They describe a biennial campus planning process, coordinated with the budgeting process. They also describe the incentives for initiating university planning and the necessity to link it to the decision-making process; this, in an environment where the libraries are considered administrative vs. academic units. The highlight of this paper is the authors' description of the critical outcomes of the process as related to the libraries, the refinement of the university's planning process in general, and recommendations for successful planning.

Beth Shapiro, Deputy Director at the Michigan State University Libraries, describes the environment at a major research university with a long tradition of strategic planning which did not always include the libraries. This paper is highlighted by a discussion of the effects of sharing fiscal information with staff in terms of establishing a focus on planning and a vision of the libraries.

Barbara Dewey is the Assistant to the University Librarian at the University of Iowa and she describes a planning process for the libraries which existed prior to a university-wide process. This paper chronicles integrating an existing process with a new university planning process and its highlight is a discussion of the future uses of the libraries' strategic plan.

Eileen Mulhare is the previous Director of Grants and Development at the Wayne State University Libraries. Wayne State is a major urban university and the author presents a detailed chronicle of a planning process undertaken in the absence of an overall institutional planning document. The process included the use of an external consultant/facilitator from the Association of Research Libraries. This paper should be read with the understanding that a major objective of the planning process was to produce a document for broad public dissemination.

President Martin Abegg of Bradley University, Provost Kalman Goldberg, and Librarian Ellen Watson take us through a planning process centered on the strategic vision of Bradley (a private institution) and the library's focus on information fluency. Their papers describe a planning and reorganization process which took place with a new library director. One of the more interesting requirements during this process was that "every academic and support unit was asked to evaluate itself," with the potential result that "programs not essential to the mission and of poor quality would be dropped." That did, in fact, occur. And, a central outcome of the Bradley process is that the campus strategic planning committee is now a standing committee of the University Senate. The highlight of these combined papers is the "Strategic Vision: 1997" statement on the library.

Russell Shank is the Assistant Vice Chancellor for Library and Information Services Planning at UCLA, another one of the nation's major urban universities. Russell's paper describes the planning process in a multi-campus system where nine library organizations are considered as one institutional library. The vagaries of local planning are explored here, and highlighted by the wisdom of the author on formal planning as an administrative process.

Marilyn Mitchell, Assistant Director at Denver's Auraria Library, and Rutherford Witthus, Head of Auraria's Archives and Special Collections present an excellent description of urbanism and the urban library in planning mode. The highlight of their article is a thoughtful examination of the organization values audit and environmental scan as two critical components of the planning process currently underway at their institution.

Linda Cain is the Dean and University Librarian at the University of Cincinnati and William F. Louden is the Assistant University Librarian for Planning and Budget. They discuss planning in a collective bargaining environment, where both faculty and staff are organized as established bargaining units; an environment where planning was conducted in the midst of a consultant's report which recommended the elimination of 300 positions across the University, over 10% of which were in the Libraries. Here is an example where the Libraries' strategic planning committee used an outside facilitator (again from the Association of Research Libraries) and a pre-planning retreat to kick-off the planning process in an atmosphere charged with apathy and skepticism. The authors present an excellent case study where wide-participation in the planning process was as important, or more, as the resulting document. The highlight of this article is the authors reflections on the process.

Leslie Manning is the Dean of Libraries at the University of Colorado at Colorado Spring. Her paper provides an excellent history of strategic planning and a review of the literature as related to higher education. It also describes a university system planning process in detail. The most interesting aspect here, however, is that the author (a librarian) was responsible for the entire planning process on her campus; one of four campuses in a university system.

The capstone paper is by Nancy Cline, Dean of Libraries at the Pennsylvania State University, and Salvatore Meringolo, Assistant

Dean and Head of Collections and Reference Services. They describe a planning initiative that started in the mid-80's with a new president in an environment of skepticism; likewise, an environment where most deans and administrators were unaccustomed to having their initiatives and programs subjected to committee review. This paper details an evolutionary process for planning at Penn State which the authors describe as a campus today with a "planning mentality." Readers will be interested in the administrative and organizational changes that have occurred as a result of Penn State's excellent planning process; one where resource allocations are tied directly to strategic goals. And one where the planning process has moved the libraries away from being seen as a competitive threat, to their being viewed as a partner in academic funding requests. The highlights of this article are the section on drawbacks and benefits to strategic planning, and the thoughtful suggestions in the conclusion.

This volume speaks broadly of a process that has afforded higher education, the academy, and its libraries a solid means of developing excellence in new academic areas while maintaining and improving the best of traditional disciplines and services. For those institutions represented in this publication, their initial and current planning activities have also poised them to enter a new plateau in strategic planning. Readers will note that the planning initiatives of these institutions were not limited to academic disciplines, as the complexities and challenges of higher education in this and the coming decade far transcend the traditional pathways of the academy. The most appropriate summary of the focus of this collection is again, a quote from A. Bartlett Giamatti:

> The most pressing need in higher education in the next ten years is not for management strategies. It is for debate on each campus, led by its leaders, as to what the purposes and goals of each campus are—for only in the open arrival at some shared consensus of what the contour, the shape, the tendency, of the campus or of higher education will be can the drift of higher education be halted; can the further internal fragmentation of campuses be forestalled; can the rush of special interest be reversed; can the public's faith that these places

know what they are about, know why they exist and where they are going, be restored.[5]

E. Gordon Gee
James F. Williams, II

REFERENCES

1. Giamatti, A. Bartlett. *A Free and Ordered Space: The Real World of the University*. New York: W.W. Norton, 1988. pp. 35-36.
2. Finch, Frank. *The Facts on File Encyclopedia of Management Techniques*. New York: Facts on File Publications, 1985. p. 244.
3. Keller, George. *Academic Strategy; The Management Revolution in American Higher Education*. Baltimore: The Johns Hopkins University Press, 1983. pp. 140-142.
4. Anne Woodsworth et al. "The Model Research Library: Planning for the Future." The Journal of Academic Librarianship, July 1989, pp. 132-138.
5. Giamatti, A. Bartlett. Ibid. pp. 37-38.

Strategic Planning and Management:
A Methodology for Responsible Change

James M. Rosser
James I. Penrod

SUMMARY. This article presents the rationale of a large, urban, culturally diverse, comprehensive university for adopting a formal strategic planning and management methodology. The external forces and the internal initiatives that contributed to the decision to do formal planning are listed. The planning model is described and the current status of the planning and management process is portrayed. The way in which the library fits into the campuswide process is depicted and planning and management challenges that await a new Librarian are presented. The paper concludes with observations regarding the need for a regional assessment of the potential for an electronic library consortium and the need for a National Research and Education Network.

INTRODUCTION

The California State University

The California State University (CSU) system comprises twenty campuses and over 360,000 students served by more than 38,000 faculty and staff. Together these institutions constitute the largest university in the world. The extended CSU campus stretches 1,000 miles, from Humbolt in the north to San Diego in the south. The CSU is part of the tripartite approach to public higher education in the State of California, along with the California Community Col-

James M. Rosser is President of California State University at Los Angeles. James I. Penrod is Vice President for Information Resources Management at California State University at Los Angeles.

9

lege System and the University of California System. The twenty CSU campuses enroll undergraduates from the top one-third of those completing a college bound curriculum in high school and student transfers who have successfully completed studies at a California Community College, as well as graduate students in a wide variety of disciplines.

California State University, Los Angeles

The California State University, Los Angeles (CSLA) campus, founded in 1947 by action of the California State Legislature, has become a comprehensive university offering programs in more than fifty academic and professional fields. The six schools of the University serve approximately 21,000 students distributed as follows: Business and Economics (25 percent), Natural and Social Sciences (17 percent), Health and Human Services (14 percent), Engineering and Technology (11 percent), Arts and Letters (10 percent), Education (5 percent), and other programs (18 percent). About one-third of the University's students are engaged in postbaccalaureate study.

Located in northeast Los Angeles, the primary service area for CSLA is ethnically diverse and economically mixed. It encompasses many of the Los Angeles basin's business, industry, and government districts. Cal State L.A. is, therefore, an urban, multicultural institution that is somewhat unique within the 20-campus CSU. It is perhaps the most ethnically diverse university in the nation—31 percent Caucasian, 29 percent Asian Pacific, 28 percent Hispanic, 11 percent African American, one percent American Indian and other. Almost 28 percent of the student body are not U.S. citizens, and 64 percent do not speak English as their primary language. Some 58 percent of students are women, 68 percent work, and the average age is 27 years.

CSLA is a quarter system, year round operation campus. There are approximately 1,300 full- and part-time faculty members and 933 full-time staff. The annual operating budget (FY'90) is $127,000,000.

FACTORS LEADING TO A FORMALIZED STRATEGIC PLANNING AND MANAGEMENT PROCESS

It has been said that the catalysts for change in higher education are reasonably clear; they come from one of three sources. The first source is a major crisis, the second is the exertion of pressure from the outside, and the last is a vigorous farsighted (perhaps, newly arrived) leader. To paraphrase, the forces of change are crisis, lust, or good fortune.[1] All of the above, in varying degrees, contributed to the decision at CSLA to institutionalize a formal methodology for strategic planning and management.

At Cal State L.A. strategic planning and management is: (1) setting goals that match institutional activities, competencies, and resources with the external environment's present and future opportunities, demands and risks; (2) formulating alternative courses of short-term and long-term action for achieving goals; (3) selecting and implementing a best course of action, and directing and coordinating resources and activities to help assure successful performances; and (4) evaluating results to insure that goals are met and monitoring the appropriateness of the course of action and the necessity for modifications.[2]

External Elements

In 1980, Cal State L. A. began the new decade with a newly installed president and a periodic visit from the Western Association of Schools and Colleges (WASC), the regional accreditation association. Although the institution's academic accreditation was extended for a full ten year cycle, several statements in the final *WASC Report* pointed to the need for enhanced planning and for a different approach to managing the resources of the campus: (1) It was specifically noted that the academic planning process was weak. (2) The faculty needed revitalization. (3) The campus lacked hardware, software and support in the critical area of information technology to meet the needs of instruction, research and administration. (4) There were concerns regarding enrollment management. (5) There was a need to take greater advantage of the strategic location of the institution. And, (6) there was a need to pursue a vigorous community relations program.[3]

The changing demographics of Southern California and the CSLA primary service area indicated that the trend toward a highly diverse multicultural student body which began in the 1970's would continue. The rate of college-going Hispanic and African American students showed that enrollment management would be a needed endeavor. As the decade progressed and participation rates dropped, this became even more significant.

The introduction of microcomputers, the divestiture of AT&T, and the growing use of information technology in disciplines other than the hard sciences pointed to rapidly expanding needs in this area. Additionally, many deficiencies in administrative support services could be traced to the lack of adequate administrative computing systems.

The era of "less is better" and conservative national and state government fiscal policies suggested that funding sources for new initiatives or for revamping problem areas would have to come primarily from reallocation of campus resources or from non-state entities.

Given the need to address a growing list of existing difficulties, environmental challenges, technological advances, and financial constraints the following strategies were derived and put into action at Cal State L.A.

Institutional Initiatives

Efforts were aimed at capitalizing on the campus location, near downtown Los Angeles and in the midst of the dynamic, multicultural environment of Southern California. Links were established with business, government, and civic leaders. From these new contacts, a reinvigorated President's Advisory Board was formed consisting of men and women representative of the ethnic diversity of the campus. Similarly, other advisory or support groups for professional schools, development activities, etc., were formed.

The University was reorganized. The schools were redefined to encompass more logical and focused academic units. Faculty development efforts and an aggressive program to recruit, retain, and promote minority and women faculty were begun. A formal, joint agreement defining functions and responsibilities was developed and endorsed by the administration and the academic senate. The administrative structure of the campus was grouped into units reporting to the President and the Vice Presidents for Academic Affairs, Information Resources Management, Operations, and Student Affairs. A University reserve consisting of about one percent of the operating budget is set aside to address unanticipated fiscal difficulties and to provide seed funding to meet unbudgeted needs and to respond to new initiatives and opportunities.

Careful recruitment was initiated for a senior administrative team oriented to strategic planning and management and dedicated to working cooperatively to accomplish institutional goals. Over a period of five years, experienced leaders were brought together. During this period, several new deans also were hired.

A vision for the future was formulated and articulated. Succinctly stated, the CSLA mission was to combine access and equity with excellence. The scenario stressed an increase in the research, scholarly, creative and service activities of the University in accord with the charge given to the CSU in the *State Master Plan*; the development of assessment measures to ensure academic accountability; a focus on the arts reflective of the cultural diversity and creativity of the service area; the provision of programs to meet the needs of elementary and secondary education into the next century; an improvement in student services; increasing effectiveness in the use of resources; building an information technology infrastructure to advance the teaching, research and public service missions of the University; and the development of a strategic planning and management methodology.

THE PLANNING MODEL

In early 1985, the President appointed a representative Long Range Planning Committee chaired by the Vice President for Academic Affairs and charged it to research and develop a planning process for CSLA. A grant of $25,000 was secured from the ARCO Foundation, with the assistance of a member of the President's Advisory Board, to underwrite expenses associated with developing the planning procedure. Over a period of several months, half a dozen planning experts from higher education were brought to the campus to describe methodologies and to provide insight into planning perspectives.

The Plan-to-Plan

By Fall 1986, several significant decisions were made and the objectives of the process were clarified: (1) The process should be evolutionary rather than revolutionary. (2) It should promote change within the institution through the normal decision making structure. (3) Planning should be focused on decisions and actions rather than on documents. (4) The process should allow some flexibility and encourage innovation. (5) It should link unit plans with individual work plans. And, (6) it should be linked to the resource allocation process.

A planning model was chosen and adapted to the CSLA environment. The Shirley Model, developed for colleges and universities, best fit the objectives.[4] The original planning committee had been reconstituted to provide an oversight and review function. It would be co-chaired by the Provost and Vice President for Academic Affairs and the Vice President for Information Resources Management. Members of the senior administration were assigned responsibility for drafting planning documents and for designing feedback loops to ensure appropriate input and evaluation.

A document was provided and widely disseminated across campus that gave an overview of common planning pitfalls, listed what had been done to date, spelled out the elements of the planning model, and specified the next steps to be taken.[5] This was the "Plan-to-Plan."

Redefining the Mission

The Long Range Planning Committee had completed an external environment analysis identifying forces in the economic, social, technological, political and legal, demographic, and competitive areas that presented specific opportunities, threats, and constraints to the institution. That Committee also had drafted a new institutional statement of fundamental purpose.

The Shirley Model and the CSLA Plan-to-Plan called for an internal strengths and weaknesses analysis and an institutional values assessment to be done in addition to the environmental analysis. The pertinent findings from the external environmental scan, the internal strengths and weaknesses analysis, and the values assessment would contribute to the development of an extended mission statement for CSLA.

The *Institutional Goals Inventory*[6] developed by the Educational Testing Service was used for the values assessment. This standardized instrument captures perceptions of respondents toward goals in a variety of areas common in colleges and universities. For each question, respondents note their perceptions of "what is" and "what should be." The analysis allows for comparisons between institutional subgroups, e.g., administrators, full time faculty, part time faculty, staff, students, etc.; as well as comparisons with sets of other institutions, e.g., public comprehensive universities, research universities, etc. The questionnaire also allowed for twenty institution specific questions to be included.

Two Blue Ribbon Committees, one composed primarily of senior faculty supplemented by senior administrators, the other composed primarily of senior administrators supplemented by senior faculty, conducted the institutional strengths and weaknesses assessment. The first group focused on broad academic areas of the University (the Schools and the Library) and the second group examined the major administrative areas (areas reporting to executive officers). The Strategic Planning Coordination Committee (SPCC) provided general guidelines for the process. The Blue Ribbon Committees drafted their reports, shared them with the appropriate dean or senior administrator, then finalized the reports, taking into consideration any feedback received. If desired, the response from the dean or senior administrator was also included with the final report.

The SPCC was responsible for drafting the extended mission statement. It contained a statement of fundamental purpose, a definition of the primary service area, a focus on the basic programs of the campus, a reference to the institution's clientele, a listing of co-curricular activities, a commitment to ethical behavior, a collegial governance structure, and adherence to academic freedom and professional ethics. The extended mission statement, supplemented with 26 statements of relative emphasis which stressed priorities, pointed out special characteristics of the institution, and further differentiated CSLA advantages. The extended mission was reviewed by the full Academic Senate, recommended to and approved by the President.

The *Strategic Plan for California State University, Los Angeles* contains a message from the President which provides an annual focus for the campus; an introduction, which relates the campus planning process to current initiatives; the extended mission and statements of relative emphasis, which provide a baseline to which all decisions should be contrasted for basic integrity; and 17 goals, which spell out accomplishments envisioned by CSLA over the next five to ten years. The first *Strategic Plan* was issued in Fall 1988, and is updated annually.

Tactical Plans

Tactical plans provide strategies and how those strategies will be implemented in specific areas which relate to the entire institution. A bridge between the strategic decision areas called for in the *Strategic Plan* and specific actions that are in unit plans is also provided. Nine tactical planning areas have been defined at CSLA. The tactical plans are derived under the direction of executive officers who have primary responsibility for implementation.

The plans and those responsible for them are as follows: (1) An academic affairs plan is provided by the Provost and Vice President for Academic Affairs. (2 and 3) The Vice President for Student Affairs provides an enrollment management plan and a student services plan. (4, 5 and 6) The Vice President for Operations is responsible for a facilities master plan, a financial plan, and a human resources management plan. (7) An information resources management plan is generated by the Vice President for IRM. (8 and 9) Finally, the President has responsibility for the development of the public affairs/community relations, including fundraising, plan and the organizational master plan.

Although considerable flexibility in format is permitted, the tactical plans generally contain most of the following elements: a short mission statement, a trends section, goals (five year horizon statements), objectives (measurable, behaviorally oriented statements of accomplishment tied to the current fiscal year), and a budget. Lengthy documents are discouraged, five to eight pages are typical.

A wide variety of processes are utilized to secure input and feedback on the tactical plans. For instance, the Provost and Vice President for Academic Affairs works with a standing committee of the Academic Senate, the Educational Policy and Resources Committee, in addition to deans and other academic administrators in developing the annual academic affairs plan. The Vice President for IRM works with three representative advisory committees in redrafting the information resources management plan. All of the tactical plans, however, are reviewed by the SPCC before going to the President for final approval. The SPCC looks for areas where cooperation and coordination will be needed to accomplish objectives; it tries to ensure that tactical goals relate directly to institutional goals, and that tactical objectives are measurable.

Tactical plans were first drafted in 1988 but, due to several iterations of modification, they were not approved until they had been updated for 1989.

Unit Plans

The *CSLA Strategic Plan* defines the idealized institution of the future and sets the highest priorities for the institution. The nine tactical plans provide broad strategies for reaching that defined future and begin to translate the priorities to budget items. Finally, the unit plans define actions to be taken within a budget cycle which, over time, result in the accomplishment of institutional goals.

As in the case of tactical plans, there is flexibility in format for unit plans. Basically the same elements as tactical plans are included, but usually are slightly shorter in length. There is also flexibility in defining what constitutes a unit. For example, Schools are defined as units and all Deans develop a unit plan. Some Deans also encourage departments to develop unit plans, others do not.

It must be noted that constraints reflected at the strategic or institutional level *and* at the tactical or functional level must also be recognized at the unit or operational level.[7] It is very important to avoid pie-in-the-sky suggestions for actions at this level, but it may be just as important to entertain at least some "dreams" for resolving issues or building for the future.[8] The goal here is to strike a workable balance between being realistic and practical, while maintaining the freedom to be innovative.

The SPCC does not review unit plans. Typically they are derived by the unit, and reviewed and approved by the administrator to whom the unit reports.

Strategic planning does not mean having a blueprint for every action or casting all strategies, tactics and actions in concrete. It is an effort to encourage all who make decisions within the organization to do so with the fate of the institution in mind.[9] The planning model utilized at CSLA is depicted in Figure 1.

The Management Link

As noted previously in this paper, the methodology employed at Cal State L.A. incorporates both planning and management. They are viewed and practiced as being different sides of the same coin. Planning documents are prepared by those who have the responsibility to see that the plans are implemented and that goals and objectives are achieved.

Goals and objectives in unit plans roll up in support of the goals and objectives in the tactical plans. They, in turn, support the long term institutional goals in the *Strategic Plan*. Each CSLA administrator is required to have an annual work plan that specifies his/her duties through measurable objectives. The objectives in these work plans tie directly to the objectives contained in the unit or tactical plans of the responsible individual. Administrators are evaluated annually based upon accomplishments associated with their work plans. Thus, results oriented planning has a direct link to salary recommendations. Since all salary increases for administrators are merit based, the process provides significant accountability.

Various methods of evaluation are utilized to ensure that services are viewed as satisfactory by those for whom the services are provided. Several administrative departments have monthly processes which provide on-going analysis of performance as judged by their client community. Others conduct periodic surveys associated with quarter registration cycles, etc., to determine perceptions of the quality of service. Some conduct departmental reviews utilizing a small evaluation team composed of individuals from outside the department being assessed. In all cases, the outcome of the process leads to the establishment of a list of action items. If a need for major change is indicated, this would usually result in objectives being incorporated in unit plans and in administrative work plans. All academic departments undergo periodic program review with involvement from discipline consultants outside the University. As with administrative units, results culminate in objectives in unit plans or, if of significant magnitude, in the *Academic Affairs Tactical Plan*.

Additionally, some service units prepare annual reports which are widely distributed and discussed by advisory committees. A university-wide annual report is provided by the Vice President for Operations. Finally, the SPCC critiques the accomplishments that result from each of the tactical plans for the campus and makes recommendations for the next iteration of the various plans based upon that analysis and generally perceived needs of the University.

STATUS OF THE PLANNING AND MANAGEMENT PROCESS

Process Outcomes

As many have noted, the process of planning and management is more important than the end product documents. It is the process that affects the bottom line of planning and management — decision-making. After experiencing two iterations of the annual planning process, some of the benefits are beginning to become evident. There are four very important organizational functions that have been substantially enhanced through the process of strategic planning at CSLA.

First, there is the role of direction and control, which leads to the implementation of the strategic vision of the plan through the development of objectives linked to the budget.[10] Providing a formal link-

FIGURE 1. Strategic Planning Model for California State University, Los Angeles

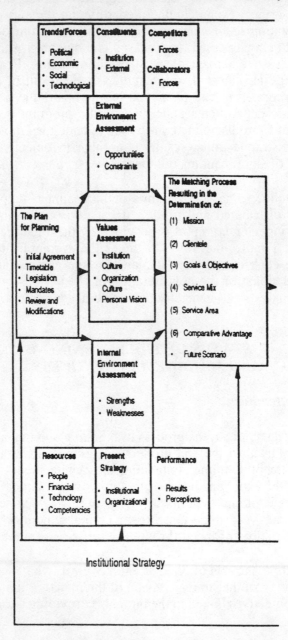

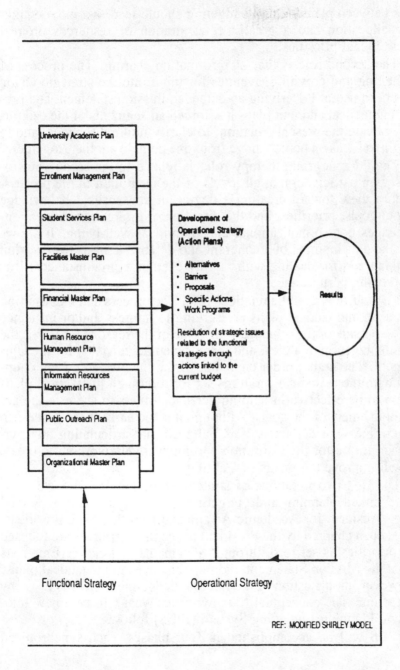

Functional Strategy   **Operational Strategy**

REF: MODIFIED SHIRLEY MODEL

age between planning and budgeting should lead to a more equitable allocation and a greater concentration of resources on real institutional priorities.[11]

The second role is that of information sharing. The process of soliciting and providing avenues for input into the strategic vision has been useful.[12] Deriving an extended mission statement and preparing tactical and unit plans has forced all segments of the campus to evaluate the present situation, to clarify future directions, and to begin to focus on how to move from one point to another, together.[13]

The third, a group therapy role, is related to the second but focuses on participation at all levels of the institution in the process, with a view toward creating a degree of consensus.[14] Knowledge about goals, priorities, and the direction of future development encourages both organizational and individual well-being. It allows for the development of a coherent and defensible basis for decision making and for dealing with rapidly changing circumstances. It is improving performance.[15]

The fourth is a public relations role. The process and the resulting strategic and tactical plans are serving to impress and/or influence those outside of the organization.[16] One of the reasons for this is the communication of a clear and inspiring strategic vision for the University. The higher order challenges from the *Strategic Plan* coupled with the realistic aspirations set forth through the tactical plans seem to be effective in helping persuade others to share in the accomplishment of the goals. Although it is too early in the process to determine with certainty, it is believed that articulating an envisioned future for the institution and innovatively working to create it will improve the image of Cal State L.A.[17]

The first two iterations of strategic planning at Cal State L.A. have linked planning and budgeting informally. The Provost and Vice President for Academic Affairs and the other Vice Presidents have been charged by the President to see that resources are focused on priorities as set forth through Statements of Relative Emphasis from the Mission Statement and the objectives in the tactical plans. However, modification of the internal budgeting system is just now occurring. The conceptual framework for what will be a new Integrated Planning Budgeting System (IPBS) follows.

IPBS will be accomplished in four phases, each synchronized

with the Academic Calendar. The first phase — strategic planning — will be conducted in the Fall Quarter and includes the review and revision of the *CSLA Strategic Plan* and the nine campus tactical plans. The second phase — unit planning/budgeting — will be conducted during the Winter Quarter and includes the development of both unit plans and budget requests. The third phase — synthesis — will be conducted during the Spring Quarter and includes the integration of unit budgets into a campus budget and the extraction and submission of numerous State and CSU reports and requests. The fourth phase — evaluation — will be conducted during the Summer Quarter and consists of an evaluation by the President and each of the Vice Presidents regarding institutional and unit objectives each area achieved in the prior fiscal year and serves as input to the next cycle of IPBS.

The strategic planning phase is initiated by the President in September. The SPCC reviews the *Strategic Plan* document and recommends changes to the President. Changes regarding the Mission or Statements of Relative Emphasis are referred to the Academic Senate for review. The SPCC finalizes the *Strategic Plan* for approval by the President. The approved plan is sent to the nine tactical planning groups. Each tactical planning group reviews its tactical plan with respect to changes over the previous year and changes in the *Strategic Plan*. The tactical plans are reviewed by the SPCC, finalized and sent to the President for approval by the end of the Fall Quarter.

Unit planning/budgeting follows the strategic phase during the Winter Quarter and involves the development of unit plans which include annual budget requests. Based on the input described above and other sources as appropriate, the President develops an IPBS initiation memo which sets the institutional priorities for the coming year. In accord with University policy, the IPBS initiation memo will be reviewed by academic governance. The unit plans must also include requests and proposals for Lottery Funds, Instructionally Related Activities, Major and Minor Capital Outlay, Program Change Proposals, Revenue Projections, etc. Unit plans are then integrated into five divisional plans — Office of the President, Academic Affairs, Operations, Information Resources Management, and Student Affairs.

During Spring Quarter the divisional plans are synthesized into a campus budget for review and approval. Requests for Lottery Funds, Instructionally Related Activities, and General Fund resources are compiled and submitted to appropriate campus committees. Major and Minor Capital Outlay, Special Repairs, Program Change Proposals, various budget formula components, Revenue Projections, and the *Campus Information Resource Plan* are compiled and submitted to the Chancellor's Office.

The President and each Vice President conduct a formal evaluation of both instructional and unit objectives and the results are reported to the campus during the Summer Quarter in an *Annual Report*. Evaluations provide information which is available for use during the next strategic planning phase the following Fall Quarter.[17]

Institutional Goals and Initiatives

As the planning process has evolved over a five-year period at CSLA, three areas of broadbased strategic initiatives have emerged. The theme of "cultural diversity and quality education" depicts the very heart and soul of the institution. It is addressed in the Extended Mission Statement, and elaborated upon in the Statements of Relative Emphasis. Eight of the 17 institutional goals address this focus.

The cultural diversity of the student body reflects, as it should, the primary service area of this urban, comprehensive, regional, public university. A number of projects are in progress helping to ensure that quality education does occur. These include: (1) a campus-based program to recruit highly qualified minority and women faculty so there will be a closer alignment between the cultural diversity of the faculty and that of the student body. In three years, almost 400 individuals nearing completion of terminal degrees have been personally contacted, another 300 have been identified, and 47 women or minorities have been employed by the University. (2) The campus played the leading role in developing a systemwide financial plan and program to assist underrepresented women and minorities in completing doctoral work. Aid is given in return for a commitment to teach in the system for a specified time. Over 200 individuals are now in the Forgiveable Loan Program. (3) A Center for Effective Teaching, based in the School of Education, has been established. Workshops, seminars, short courses, and personal analysis, along with a wealth of resource materials are available. The general focus is on the improvement of classroom instruction with emphasis on teaching a diverse student body. (4) A variety of successful programs, some specifically directed to minority students, designed to encourage undergraduate participation in research are ongoing. (5) All undergraduates are required to pass a Writing Proficiency Examination before becoming eligible to graduate. Work continues to improve the process and to provide more effective help to those who have difficulty in meeting this standard. And, (6) an annual one day symposium is sponsored by the President, the Provost and Vice President for Academic Affairs, and the Academic Senate for all faculty. Specific topics relate to diversity and quality and experts are brought in to share perspectives with CSLA faculty and other members of the University community.

Cal State L.A. has been designated as a focal point for the Arts within the CSU by the Chancellor. A campus goal is "to become a focal point in the Arts reflective of the cultural diversity and creativity of the University and the community."[18] Initiatives that are helping to bring this about are: (1) The establishment of a School of Arts and Letters; implementation of a MFA degree in Art; establishment of a Department of Theatre Arts and Dance; securing state funding for remodeling fine arts facilities and non-state funding for a state-of-the-art dance complex. (2) In 1986, the Los Angeles County High School for the Arts opened on the CSLA campus. This county-wide comprehensive high school enrolls artistically talented students who are as a body ranked in the top two percent of high school students in the State of California. Programs have been initiated which allow students to take college level courses for credit prior to graduation. (3) In 1989, Cal State L.A. became the summer home for the renowned Joffrey Ballet. While the company is on campus, a rich interchange between University faculty and students and the Joffrey artists takes place. And, (4) ground breaking for the Harriet and Charles Luckman Fine Arts Complex will occur in early 1990. This 21 million dollar complex will be the first of its kind in the CSU, containing a 1200 seat main theatre. Through an innovative funding arrangement, the campus will raise approximately one third of the costs from private sources, and the State will provide the remainder. When completed in 1992, this state-of-the-art complex will showcase the arts reflecting diverse cultural perspectives and will provide education, entertainment and cultural enjoyment for the campus and surrounding community.

It is clear that the emerging global society of the information age requires graduates from higher education who can competently utilize information technology within their discipline if they are to be professionally successful. With this in mind, CSLA strives "to advance the teaching, research, and public service missions of the University through the application of state-of-the-art technology and information management, thus providing a model for comprehensive universities."[19] The following actions have been taken in support of this goal.

An information resources management (IRM) approach to dealing with technology and information management was initiated in 1985. An IRM unit was created incorporating all major information resource functions within the University except for the Library. The unit was led by a newly named Vice President with responsibility for all issues related to information technology. In 1986 the *CSLA Campus Information Resources Plan* was the first formal output resulting from the strategic planning methodology. It called for the IRM unit to (1) plan, coordinate and assist faculty in building an academic computing infrastructure to meet the needs of CSLA through the 1990's; (2) plan, justify, procure, install and operate a state-of-the-art telecommunications system and campuswide network; and (3) plan, design, procure, install and operate integrated, relational based administrative applications systems.[20]

In Fall 1986, the CSLA academic computing environment consisted of about 400 student workstations/terminals in 14 labs or classrooms with 2 LANs, 60 faculty workstations, 14 mini/super minicomputers, a Cyber 730 (shared with administrative computing), 200 ports on a Gandalf PACX system, 4 full-time support staff, and about 20 student assistants. In Fall 1989, the academic information technology environment had 630 student workstations in 33 labs or classrooms with 16 LANs, approximately 360 faculty workstations, 28 mini/super minicomputers, an Alliant mini supercomputer, 340 ports on two Gandalfs and an Infotron INX with a bridge to a Proteon Pronet-10, 17 full-time support staff (11 in Academic Technology Support and 6 in Schools/Departments) and 45 student assistants. Additionally, annual academic information technology donations to the campus have tripled to over one million dollars.

A Pacific Bell Central Office Centrex providing approximately 2225 telephones, coupled with a Gandalf PACX port selector based data network with about 450 connections, comprised the communications resources for CSLA in Fall 1986. The campus now has a telecommunications system from Centel Communications Systems consisting of a Northern Telecom Meridian SL-1 PBX with about 2670 telephones, an Infotron INX 4400 medium speed data switch with 250 connections, a Proteon Pronet-10 fiber optic high speed network which supports Ethernet, Token Ring, Starlan 3BNet and Appleshare LANs, a Digital Sound voice server with 555 voice mail boxes, and ComSoft system management software running on a Microvax 3600. Additionally, the Gandalf PACX with approximately 750 connections is linked to the Infotron INX.

The administrative computing environment in Fall 1986 consisted of a variety of CSU developed Cobol systems, and an Information Associates (IA) integrated business system/financial accounting system (that was significantly modified), operating on the campus Cyber 730. The majority of applications were batch processing, and there was little integration between different modules. There were about 250 administrative connections on the the Gandalf. Today, through project OASIS, a joint development project between IBM, IA, CSLA, California State University, Long Beach, and Cal Poly San Luis Obispo, the institution has the alumni development system (ADS), the financial records system (FRS) (with a CSU developed front end), and the student information system (SIS) from IA Series Z applications. A few other Cobol administrative applications have been converted and a property management system has been developed in FOCUS. All applications now run on an IBM 4381 T92E. The Series Z applications are fully integrated and provide on-line access to about 700 administrative users and academic departments.[21] Beta testing of the IA modules in IBM's DB2 relational database will begin later this year.

PARTICIPATION OF THE LIBRARY
IN THE PROCESS

The Library Plan

The John F. Kennedy Memorial Library at Cal State L.A. is one of the seven major academic units reporting to the Provost and Vice President for Academic Affairs. Like the Schools of the University, it has developed a unit plan responding to the needs of the campus with focus provided primarily through priorities set forth in goals and objectives contained in the *Academic Tactical Plan*.

Again, like the Schools, priorities in information technology for the Library are also shaped by goals and objectives contained in the *IRM Tactical Plan*. Three important projects relate to the IRM Plan. (1) The networking thrust is exhibited by all professional staff now having voice mail and electronic mail access to campus resources. A LAN with a bridge to the campus backbone is planned that will provide high speed data transmission rates where necessary. (2) A pilot project utilizing a CD-ROM database and linking it to the campus network is underway. And, (3) a major project to procure and install an online public access catalog (OPAC) system has begun.

The Need for a Strategic Assessment
of Role and Functions

This is a critical time for the Library at CSLA. A search is in progress for a new University Librarian. That individual needs the vision to lead the transformation of what has been a good traditional library, with a focus on being a caretaker of information, to the library of the next century with an emphasis on access and delivery of information.[22]

Historically, librarians have been concerned with the need to acquire, catalog, organize, store, retrieve, and otherwise cope with the tasks dealing with the containers of information and knowledge. Indeed, this need will continue whether dealing with materials in paper, video, audio, optical, magnetic, or other media. The historical presumption, however, that "knowledge" in formally recorded media such as paper, photographs, and so on, has a more valued status than "soft" materials such as computer printouts or information in on-line databases that may be updated in real time, is proving to be incorrect. As more and more decisions, research, and learning depend on information with an increasingly short half-life, the role of the librarian moves closer to that of information manager. That is, the librarian must be concerned with end results, not just with citations and locations and with providing information to end users that help bring about positive consequences.[23]

This concept, coupled with the widely recognized necessity for libraries to become "multimedia switching points" and perhaps the major node on a campus network, points to building a true and steadfast partnership between libraries and computing and communications units. At CSLA, this will mean that the Library must work more closely and effectively with IRM to develop strategies and tactics that will be reflected in the *IRM Tactical Plan* — a plan to provide campuswide parameters for the development of "centers for electronically managed information, knowledge, and publishing support activities."[24]

A second and perhaps more critical issue is for the Library to become a demand-driven organization rather than one that is supply oriented. Currently, most libraries are expensive, supply oriented entities; they buy a supply of materials and place them on shelves. If customers want to use them, they search catalogs and indexes, go to the shelves, take what they find to the check-out counter, and hope that it serves their needs.[25]

Changes in technology, user attitudes and expectations are causing libraries to become demand-driven. Providing customized electronic services for specific information will increasingly become a necessity if users are to be satisfied. Such a change requires librarians to take a fresh look at what they do. They will need to ask questions such as: "What are the common characteristics of groups of users? What are their needs? What elements of service are of greatest importance to users? How should strategic services be designed, marketed, and delivered? Where will investments be made? How will quality and costs be controlled? How are the components and characteristics of service best matched with the needs of customers?" A far more perplexing question is: How can we effectively utilize other libraries and information resources within a system, state, region, nation, etc., respectively? As expectations change, libraries must focus less on what is thought to be good for people or what is on the shelves and more on needs as defined by the customer.[26]

Next Steps

Whomever accepts the responsibility of becoming the new Librarian at Cal State L.A. will have a significant agenda to address, as do others in similar roles. That agenda includes the major issues just discussed: (1) transforming the library from that of a caretaker of information to an organization with emphasis on access and delivery of information; and, (2) moving the library from a supply-oriented organization to a demand-driven unit. Additional topics include: (3) problems, policies, and issues concerned with information in electronic format such as: copyright; freedom of access; ownership; author compensation and fair use; standards; site licenses which enable cooperative ventures, etc.;[27] (4) deriving strategies to address resource issues, both the reallocation of existing resources and identification of additional resources; (5) serving as the point of contact and coordinator for joint efforts with the CSU system and/or other state, regional, national etc., entities; (6) seeking and exploring opportunities with information product vendors to serve as a test site for research and development; and (7) addressing the in-service and pre-service needs of professional librarians.

The process of strategic planning and management in place at CSLA should assist the individual selected in many ways. Careful analysis of the existing *Library Unit Plan* should provide significant insight into the perceptions, organizational culture, and present strategies of the staff. Conducting an external and internal environmental scan with a values assessment will enable the new Librarian to focus on opportunities, constraints, strengths and weaknesses to determine where changes are needed in organizational behaviors, fiscal support, and where personal vision will need to be articulated. Redefining the mission statement, projecting a future scenario, and deriving new goals and objectives through group activities can refine and reorient the culture of the organization and develop a new teamwork approach to planning and problem solving inclusive of the existing IRM unit.

CONCLUDING OBSERVATIONS

Needs Beyond the Campus

The dream of building an electronic library to bring to a scholar's desk all the information that is needed for research, scholarship and creative activities is more than 20 years old, but is only now becoming a reality with a feasible demonstration through the Carnegie Mellon University and OCLC Project Mercury.[28] Examining different implementations of the electronic library vision shows that what emerges is not just a local collection of hardware and software with information stored electronically or optically, but a network of information tools and services.[29] When one begins to envision an electronic library within the context of the CSU, the idea of a coordinated network immediately comes to mind.

Many issues would need to be overcome to consider realistically the possibility of a coordinated CSU electronic library network. Some illustrative examples are: How would direct and easy access for users be provided, given different systems are in place? How would costs be shared? What about declining autonomy at the local institution? How would the network make decisions? What role should the Chancellor's Office play? What resource trade-offs versus other systemwide needs would have to be made? What campus policies would need to be re-examined? Which databases would be available? How would membership be determined? Who would initiate and lead the project?[30]

Although these and many other such issues are far from being trivial, potential advantages are great enough that consideration should be given to conducting a feasibility study. In the long run, building an infrastructure to share electronic information and databases across a 20-campus system, thus eliminating substantial duplication, would seem to have economic and practical benefit. A systemwide data network is already in place and upgrades to support high speed file transmission are being planned. The Computing and Communications Resource unit in the Chancellor's Office is charged with coordinating information technology projects, including libraries. Therefore, the authors encourage exploration of the potential for a CSU electronic library.

Looking beyond the CSU to the State of California, the region and to the nation, the greatest immediate need may be to establish a National Research and Education Network. Such a network would not only provide the magnet to pull multimedia resources together, it would amplify the promise of the new technology.[31] Indeed, it may be necessary if the United States is to maintain international competitiveness and the viability of American jobs in the future. The proposed network would serve education, industry and government and would: "(1) Increase technology transfer from basic research discoveries to usable products and services; (2) Provide researchers and educators uniform access to national information resources, regardless of their institution's size or location; (3) Stimulate the creation of important information resources such as databases, high technology instruments, and computation centers; (4) Act as a catalyst for development of advanced American networking technologies and services; and (5) Create a cohesive national research and education computer network architecture — an architecture that will evolve gracefully to meet capacity, connectivity, security, usability, management and service requirements."[32]

Colleges and universities of all sizes, in every state, could access high performance computing tools, data banks, super computers, libraries, specialized research facilities, and educational technology presently available to only a few large universities and laboratories. Development of the project requires executive level and legislative leadership; core funding from the federal government; network management by partners in the endeavor; continued research into advanced networking technologies; expansion of existing networks such as NSFnet; continued development of regional networks; and campus-based networks to link faculty and students to the National Research and Education Network.[33]

The time is now right to bring about change in a responsible manner. Electronic libraries and networked information technologies will change the world in the 1990s. While some change will be predictable, some will not because these technologies are intimately tied to basic organizational and social structures of instruction, research, scholarly and creative activities.[34] Clearly, effective and efficient implementation of these technologies requires planning, and the future of our institutions calls for that planning to be strategic, and for change, anticipated or not, to be strategically managed.

NOTES

1. George Keller, *Academic Strategy: The Management Revolution in American Higher Education*, (Baltimore and London: Johns Hopkins University Press, 1983), 164.

2. Mark Meredith, Robert G. Cope, and Oscar T. Lenning, *Differentiating Bonafide Strategic Planning From Other Planning*, (A Study Paper, May 1987), 3.

3. *Report of an Evaluation Visit of California State University, Los Angeles*, (Western Association of Schools and Colleges, April 1980), 56-57.

4. Robert C. Shirley, "Strategic Planning: An Overview," *Successful Strategic Planning: Case Studies*, New Directions for Higher Education, No. 64 (San Francisco: Jossey-Bass, 1988), 11-12.

5. James I. Penrod, "A Report to the Campus: Strategic Planning at CSLA Fall 1986," (September 30, 1986), 1-11.

6. Richard E. Pearson and Normal P. Uhl, *Formulating College and University Goals: A Guide for Using the Institutional Goals Inventory*, (Princeton, New Jersey: Educational Testing Service College and University Programs, 1977), 1-91.

7. Robert C. Shirley, "Identifying the Levels of Strategy for a College or University," *Long Range Planning*, 16, No. 3, (June 1983), 97.

8. John M. Bryson, "A Strategic Planning Process for Public and Non-Profit Organizations," *Long Range Planning*, 21, No. 1, (1988), 77.

9. Keller, ibid., 140-151.

10. Langley, ibid.

11. *California State University, Los Angeles Financial Tactical Plan*, (November 1989), 5-6.

12. Langley, ibid.

13. Shirley, "Strategic Planning . . . ," ibid.

14. Langley, ibid.

15. Shirley, "Strategic Planning . . . ," ibid.

16. Ann Langley, "The Roles of Formal Strategic Planning," *Long Range Planning*, 21, No. 3, (1988), 47-48.

17. Shirley, "Strategic Planning . . . ," ibid.

18. *California State University, Los Angeles Strategic Plan*, Goal G, (October 1989), 11.

19. Ibid, Goal P, 12.

20. James I. Penrod and Michael G. Dolence, "The Best Laid Plans — An Implementation Perspective," *Proceedings of the 1989 CAUSE National Conference*, (Boulder, CO: December 1989), in press.

21. Ibid.

22. Donald A. Marchand, "IMR Interview: W. David Penniman," *Information Management Review*, 3, No. 4, (1988), 72-73.

23. Forest Woody Horton, Jr., "Librarianship and Information Management," *Information Management Review*, 4, No. 1, (Summer 1988), 62-63.

24. Anne Woodsworth and James F. Williams II, "Computer Centers and

Libraries: Working Toward Partnerships," *Library Management and Administration*, (March 1988), 89.

25. Miriam A. Drake, "From Print to Non-Print Materials: Library Information Delivery Systems," *Educom Bulletin*, 23, No. 1, (Spring 1988), 29.

26. Ibid.

27. Anne Woodsworth, "Computing Centers and Libraries as Cohorts: Exploiting Mutual Strengths," *Computing, Electronic Publishing and Information Technology*, (The Haworth Press, Inc. 1988), 23.

28. William Y. Arms and Lisa D. Holzhauser, "Mercury: an Electronic Library," *OCLC Newsletter*, (September/October 1988), 15.

29. Mark Kibbey and Nancy H. Evans, "The Network is the Library," *EDUCOM Review*, 24, No. 3, (Fall 1989), 15.

30. Anne Woodsworth, "The Impact of Globalizing a Campus Library," *CAUSE/EFFECT*, 12, No. 2, (Summer 1989), 45.

31. Kenneth M. King, "The Multimedia Revolution," *Information Technology Quarterly*, 8, No. 4, (Winter 1989), 5.

32. *NREN: The National Research and Education Network*, (The Coalition for the National Research and Education Network, Washington, D.C., 1989), 5.

33. Ibid., 15.

34. Clifford A. Lynch, "Library Automation and the National Research Network," *EDUCOM Review*, 24, No. 3, (Fall 1989), 26.

Strategic Planning at Iowa State University: Affirmation and Expectations

Gordon P. Eaton
Jean W. Adams

SUMMARY. The process, results and status of academic strategic planning at Iowa State University are described. The president initiated strategic planning in 1987 as the mechanism by which to establish major future emphases and directions for the university within the context of its significantly changing external environment. University-wide goals, objectives and strategies were developed for the teaching, research and outreach functions of the institution. Each academic program was reviewed and formal recommendations (some of them controversial) were made for program enhancement, reorganization and institutional consolidation. Changes are now being implemented, including the adoption of ongoing strategic planning and program review.

I. THE DECISION TO ENGAGE IN STRATEGIC PLANNING

In June, 1986, the 11th president of Iowa State University, Dr. W. Robert Parks, retired following more than two decades of salutary leadership. He had ably guided the institution through significant eras of challenge and change and had effectively managed diversification of the institution, its basic organizational structure and its academic curricula. He had also overseen momentous growth in

---

Gordon P. Eaton is President of Iowa State University of Science and Technology at Ames, IA. Jean W. Adams is Associate Provost of Iowa State University of Science and Technology at Ames, IA.

35

the institutional budget and capital facilities, as well as in the size of the student body.

The last seven years of President Parks' term of office were difficult ones, however, for the state had entered a protracted period of rapid economic decline and hardship. Iowa is one of America's premiere agricultural states, but it is also one whose economy is still far too heavily dependent on the agricultural enterprise. The impact of the farm crisis of the 1980's on the whole of the state was devastating. Public higher education was in no way spared. Five times between 1979 and 1986 the state was forced to engage in budget reversions that, in the aggregate, hacked nearly $20 million from the operating budget base of the university.

Three other phenomena, two of them necessitated by continuing revenue shortfalls, added to the institution's difficulties: the inability of the state to continue to support the variable costs of its public university students' educations and its incapacity to maintain competitive faculty and staff salaries, which resulted in a hemorrhaging loss of senior faculty who left for "greener pastures" at universities in other states. The third phenomenon, in the best of times a happy circumstance, was continued rapid growth in the student body. From 1979 to 1986, years in which the institutional budget declined in constant dollar terms, the enrollment at Iowa State grew by 3,100 students, putting further severe strains on the institution's increasingly limited resources.

One measure of the extremity of the state's circumstances in attempting to continue to fund higher education is the fact that Iowa only had need to support three public, four-year institutions. Unlike neighboring states, and others across the country, it had exercised caution, prudence and restraint during the baby-boom years and chosen not to build additional campuses that would have been a further drain on resources at this time. Despite the correctness of its actions in this regard, even three institutions turned out to be a severe financial burden to attempt to maintain.

It was against the backdrop of these events, events lasting nearly a decade, if one includes the last several years of the decade of the 1970's, because of the severe rate of double digit inflation at that time, that the succeeding administration decided to engage in a strategic planning exercise aimed at two rather specific goals: first, attempting to restore, early on, a rational working balance to the relationship between the university's limited operating resources and the sum of what it was attempting to deliver to students and other clientele; and second, devoting serious and immediate attention to the means of restoring an admittedly flagging academic quality and reputation.

Recent models of strategic planning processes at other academic institutions were reviewed at the outset of Iowa State's effort. The new president had recently engaged in such a process at another institution. There, the planning body had been dominated by members of the central administration, but the financial circumstances and objectives were sufficiently different at Iowa State so that, in the end, a wholly different approach was embraced. Accordingly, it was decided to begin the planning process from the institutional base with the appointment of an ad hoc advisory committee made up primarily of senior members of the faculty, with several additional members from the professional and scientific staff and the student body. Following consultation with a wide constituency across campus with respect to the nominating process, a planning committee of 21 members was seated in May of 1987. In seeking nominations for membership on this committee, the president indicated publicly that what he sought were statesman-like individuals who would be willing to take part in protracted rational discussions of the possible elimination of their own academic units.

In the early stages of the review and planning process, the president met twice with the full committee, indicating his permanent "on-call availability" at such times as the committee wished to consult him or obtain his reactions to the directions it was taking. As the planning process proceeded, he met a dozen times or more with committee members, sometimes in groups that represented specific subcommittees, sometimes with separate individuals, most frequently with the chairperson. It was understood that the president's principal role, as well as that of the provost and the academic deans, was to begin at a point much later in the process, after the committee had completed its environmental scans and program reviews and had drawn up a set of preliminary recommendations.

In his initial charge to the Long-Range Strategic Planning Committee (Section II) the president expressed his desire to have them sketch out a draft design for a future for the institution that was different from the present and to develop proposals that would serve as guidelines for the university's immediate and intermediate future. It was suggested, on the basis of both demographic and revenue projections, that it would be a somewhat smaller institution with perhaps fewer resources, but one that should be stronger as a result of sharper academic focus.

The president indicated to the committee that it must identify and seize upon the areas of the university's greatest and most extraordinary strengths and promises, and must begin to concentrate on these areas and enhance them for the benefit of its students, its faculty and the citizens who support it. He further emphasized that the committee should place no limits on the scope of its thoughts or its discussion. It was, so to say, to think ordinarily "unthinkable" thoughts and speak perhaps "unspeakable" words as it undertook its rigorous deliberations concerning the matter of sharper institutional focus. It was also instructed to develop a plan that would promote future organizational flexibility and a capacity to adapt to change, both anticipated and unanticipated.

II. COMMITTEE CHARGE

As noted, the basic charge given to Iowa State's Long-Range Strategic Planning Committee was to develop and recommend a strategic plan that would set forth major emphases and directions for Iowa State University during the next five to ten years in the context of the changing parameters of the university's environment. The committee was asked to analyze recent and projected changes in the environment external to the university and to determine current and future areas of comparative advantage for Iowa State relative to other institutions of higher education in Iowa and elsewhere. Within this context, the committee was charged with developing recommendations concerning the basic mission of the institution, its various clientele, its program and service mix, its resources and its geographic service area. Specific goals, objectives and strategies were to be developed that would position Iowa State University for continued success within the changing environment.

On the academic program level, the committee was asked to ana-

lyze the strengths and weaknesses of existing programs and to identify, separately, Iowa State's truly unique programs, those that were
state or federally mandated and in need of possible enhancement
and those that had achieved or were very close to achieving national
or international eminence. Recommendations consistent with the
university-wide goals and objectives were to be developed for program enhancement, reorganization and consolidation.

III. FACTORS INCLUDED IN THE PROCESS
OF DEVELOPING AN ACADEMIC STRATEGY
FOR THE UNIVERSITY

The detailed work of the committee began with a thorough review of the strategic planning literature and examples of strategic
plans and planning processes used at a variety of other academic
institutions. Consistent with the charge given by the president, the
planning committee focused its initial efforts on university-wide issues that relate to the essential nature and mission of the university,
its land-grant heritage, institutional strengths and weaknesses and
the external environment within which it operates. The committee
recognized that the outcome of strategic planning should be the establishment and implementation of goals, objectives and strategies
that relate the internal strengths and weaknesses and potential capabilities to the opportunities and threats that arise from perceived and
probable changes in the external environment.

Parameters and Assumptions

The president provided the committee with a one-page listing of
14 parameters and assumptions concerning the university's future.
These parameters and assumptions concerned: the nature of the university (e.g., continuation of status and obligations as a land-grant
institution and continuation of basic priorities of teaching, research
and outreach service); the comprehensive goal of the university to
achieve a level of preeminence; the commitment to expand the university's role in international affairs; five-year enrollment projections and the need to manage enrollment consistent with available
financial and facilities resources; expectations about future funding

and the need to seek increased funds from gifts, contracts and grants; and nondiscriminatory access to the university's programs and employment, with vigorous pursuit of goals to increase minority enrollments, degrees conferred and employment. While these parameters and assumptions were presented as the president's expectations, the committee was encouraged to challenge or recommend revision on the basis of the committee's findings and analyses.

Institutional Strengths and Weaknesses

During its first few months the committee discussed university-wide strengths and weaknesses as perceived by members of the committee, based on their own experiences and the results of various previous surveys of faculty, students and the general public. A preliminary list of strengths and weaknesses was developed during a vigorous brainstorming session, with subsequent additions suggested by committee members following distribution of the initial items. This generated lengthy lists of specific strengths and weaknesses, with several items appearing on both lists. The specific items were organized by area, such as undergraduate education and support services, graduate programs, research/scholarship, outreach, faculty, administration, campus/community environment and funding. Individual committee members evaluated each of the suggested strengths and weaknesses on a 10-point scale in terms of: their importance to the institution; how well Iowa State was doing relative to peer institutions; how well Iowa State was doing relative to the level to which it should aspire; and the emphasis that should be given to achieving change. The ratings were then used to rank-order the strengths and weaknesses.

The process of identifying and ranking institutional strengths and weaknesses was especially useful in helping the committee determine the most important issues to try to address through planning. At various times during the planning process, committee members re-examined the findings of the analysis of strengths and weaknesses to ensure that the most important issues were being addressed.

Land-Grant Heritage and Principles

Because of Iowa State University's historical roots and continuing status as Iowa's, as well as the nation's first, land-grant institution, the planning committee reviewed the history of the land-grant
college concept and the federal and state statutory bases and mandates for Iowa State as a land-grant university. The committee also
reviewed several articles about the contemporary meaning and role
of land-grant universities, including the widely disseminated article
"Revitalizing Land-Grant Universities" by G. Edward Schuh.[1] The
committee then developed a statement of land-grant principles to
define the application of the modern land-grant philosophy to Iowa
State University. The proposed principles concerned: access to the
university's programs; the provision of a liberal education to all
students; the integration of teaching, research and outreach and the
incorporation of international dimensions into these programs and
activities; an institutional emphasis on the discovery and creation of
basic scientific knowledge and its development and transfer to agriculture and industry; and the responsibility of the university to enhance the quality of life for the citizens of the state.

Review and Revision
of the Mission Statement

The proposed land-grant principles were used by the planning
committee as a basis for reaffirming the traditional mission of the
university and for suggesting some revisions in the university's existing mission statement to more clearly articulate appropriate institutional emphases. In particular, the planning committee endorsed
retention of the institutional emphasis on science and technology,
within the context of providing a liberal undergraduate education
and offering a broad range of high-quality undergraduate programs,
as befits the institution's stature as a university.

Review of Selected Aspects
of the External Environment

The committee reviewed information from a wide variety of
sources concerning significant social, demographic, economic, po-

litical and technological trends and changes that are occurring or are anticipated in the United States and, in some cases, worldwide. Because many of these changes could be expected to affect the university in the years ahead, the planning committee established a subcommittee to study in detail those aspects of the external environment that were identified as being particularly important to the university's future and for which the committee needed specific information. The subcommittee prepared a lengthy report that presented historical data, current figures and projections and discussed the implications for the university with respect to the following five aspects of the external environment: (1) Iowa's population and age distribution; (2) enrollment trends and projections; (3) agriculture and the impact on the largely agricultural Iowa economy; (4) Iowa's business and industry; and (5) Iowa's ability to support higher education.

The planning committee concluded that the trends and changes in the external environment within which the university functions indicate that the next ten years will be a crucial time in the history of the university. It was determined that in some cases, Iowa State University could take action to avoid or offset undesirable changes in its external environment; in other cases, perhaps, the best the university could do is to be prepared for the changes and try to minimize their adverse effects. The analysis of the external environment reinforced the need for strategic planning to help position the university for continued success and to enable it to take advantage of appropriate opportunities that arise.

The analysis of population and enrollment projections indicated that Iowa State needs to be increasingly aggressive in recruiting qualified students directly from high school and that the institution needs to make appropriate adjustments in its academic programs to make them more accessible and attractive to adult students who wish to combine higher education with full- or part-time employment. It was noted that special efforts also should be undertaken to take advantage of opportunities to increase the university's enrollment of women and minority students and to raise graduate enrollments.

The analysis of Iowa's economy helped to define the responsibility and opportunities for the university to contribute to the development and diversification of the state's economy. The study of the state's support for higher education relative to its financial base demonstrated the state's strong commitment to higher education, but it also led to the conclusion that the university cannot reasonably expect the state to provide significantly higher levels of funding. Similarly, additional increases in tuition beyond the level of inflation would harm the university's ability to recruit students and thereby generate tuition income, especially in view of the increased state and national competition for students. Such increases would also have the undesired effect of reducing access to higher education for Iowans. Thus, it was suggested that additional resources would need to be sought through gifts, contracts and grants. While increases in such external funding were believed to be likely, it was recognized that they would tend to occur as opportunities in specific disciplinary areas.

The analyses of the external environment concluded that the demographic changes and the financial circumstances facing the university indicated that the university needed to re-examine its programs and determine which ones were most central to its mission. By focusing its limited resources on the development of high-quality and nationally eminent programs that are essential to the mission, the contribution of the university to its students and the people of the state and beyond would be maximized and the overall stature of the university would be raised.

IV. DEVELOPMENT OF PROPOSED GOALS, OBJECTIVES AND STRATEGIES

The planning committee's analysis of the factors discussed above was used to develop recommended university-wide goals, objectives and strategies. The committee decided that the focus of the current planning activity needed to be on the academic areas of the institution, in particular on the teaching, research and outreach functions of the institution. The committee recognized the important role the nonacademic support areas fulfill, but concluded that an evaluation of these areas should not be undertaken until decisions were made on the major academic issues facing the institution. Thus, the committee recommended that the support units and nonacademic services be addressed in subsequent phases of strategic planning and become part of the ongoing process for strategic planning for Iowa State University. The library constitutes the critical and fundamental depository of most of the knowledge held and nurtured by the institution and, as such, it is a key element of the academic enterprise. In the initial strategic planning process undertaken at Iowa State, discussions and recommendations concerning the library were held in abeyance, awaiting a determination first of recommended programmatic emphasis and enhancement.

Within the primary goals of developing and maintaining high-quality instructional programs, basic and applied research and extension and other outreach programs, the planning committee proposed a set of specific objectives (defined as changes needed to achieve the primary goals) and strategies (the specific means by which to realize the objectives and, thereby, to attain the primary goals). In addition, the committee identified the need to achieve diversity among students and employees and suggested ways to accomplish this goal. A variety of university-wide personnel strategies were also proposed to help achieve the primary goals. The committee recommended that there be close monitoring of all aspects of the strategic plan that is adopted, and it identified some key success indicators of progress in achieving the recommended goals and objectives. The key indicators are ones that can be evaluated on an ongoing basis, most through objective quantitative measures.

The release of the report concerned with these elements, the first of two to emerge from the committee, was followed by a series of open meetings, held in November and December of 1988, for the various internal constituencies of the university. After reviewing the written comments received by the February 1, 1989, deadline, the provost held a colloquium in March 1989 to summarize and comment on the issues raised in the responses to the report. Most of the committee's recommendations, including the adoption of ongoing strategic planning and program review, were endorsed. The development and implementation of some specific proposals were postponed, however, to be coordinated with the findings and recommendations of other studies of the university that had been instituted by the Iowa Board of Regents.

V. THE REVIEW OF ACADEMIC PROGRAMS

In addition to developing university-wide goals, objectives and strategies, the planning committee also conducted a six-month review of each of the more than 200 academic programs offered by Iowa State University. The aim was to develop recommendations for program enhancement, reorganization and consolidation consistent with the university-wide goals and the reality of limited resources. The Long-Range Strategic Planning Committee established the procedures, criteria and principles for the review of academic programs; the review itself was conducted by the Academic Program Review Subcommittee, which was composed of the 13 members of the planning committee who held permanent academic rank.

The review of academic programs was based on information provided by the departments and college deans, as well as information included in various internal university reports and external reviews and surveys. Both quantitative and qualitative information was used. The committee developed department and college questionnaires to solicit specific information about program strengths, weaknesses, quality and reputation, program uniqueness, aspirations and related funding and space needs.

After reviewing the information about the programs and following meetings with each of the college deans, the subcommittee evaluated the academic programs in terms of the following five criteria: (1) centrality to the university mission; (2) quality — current and potential; (3) demand — by majors and in total; (4) comparative advantage and uniqueness (relative to programs offered at other institutions, especially those at the other two public universities in Iowa); and (5) financial considerations — costs relative to revenues.

In arriving at its recommendations for program change, the subcommittee applied principles developed for determining program priority and specific objectives that were set forth for the reorganization and consolidation of programs, departments and colleges. The specific objectives included: (1) strengthening areas of high priority for the university; (2) providing structures and resources that would facilitate identification and development of future areas of institutional priority; (3) reducing internal duplication or overlap among programs; (4) helping differentiate Iowa State's programs from those at other institutions, especially among the three public universities in Iowa; (5) reducing administrative overhead and increasing administrative efficiency; and (6) increasing instructional efficiency. Throughout its review, the subcommittee applied the perspective of what was seen as best for the university as a whole, rather than the narrower perspective of what might be best for individual programs.

Many significant and controversial changes were recommended, including the elimination of a number of departments and programs and the merger or reorganization of many other programs. Five program areas were identified for substantial university-wide enhancement during the next decade; each of these five programs was found to be central to the university's mission and in need of improvement, not only for the program's own sake, but also to achieve maximum improvement of other highly central academic programs to which it was or might be linked. Identified specifically, these programs provide clear implications that will serve as inputs for the process of planning for the university's library.

The subcommittee also recommended that every program that was to be continued should develop specific plans for program improvement, consistent with university and college plans. While such plans could include requests for additional funds, the limited flexible university resources expected to be forthcoming dictated that most program areas will need to rely on their own resources, energies and creativity to achieve appropriate improvement. The subcommittee strongly believed that the most important and essential means to improve programs was to raise the expectations of the faculty, staff, students and administration. The subcommittee argued that program improvement requires the will to effect change, accompanied by appropriate administrative leadership; it is only in some instances that additional funding is required.

The subcommittee's evaluation of and recommendations for the academic programs were included in a 115 page report that was submitted to the president and distributed to every faculty member, as well as to various other on- and off-campus constituencies. As recommended by the subcommittee, the university community and other affected constituencies were given ample opportunity to discuss the recommendations before the president and provost decided which recommendations should be implemented, which should be studied further and which should be rejected. Members of the subcommittee met with the college deans, faculty and student groups to answer questions and to clarify the recommendations. A two-month period, subsequently extended to three months, was designated for response.

Because of the focus and specificity of the report and recommendations, primary reliance was placed upon the academic colleges and departments to organize discussions of, and to prepare written responses to, the recommendations. Each college dean was asked to coordinate the review of the report within his or her college and to submit to the provost a written response to those recommendations that pertained directly to the departments and programs within the college and those recommendations for departments and programs in other colleges that were closely related to, or might have a significant effect upon, the programs of their colleges. In addition, individuals and departments, and other groups were invited to respond in writing to the provost. The provost requested that responses identify the advantages and disadvantages of the recommendations and describe preferred alternatives to achieve the goals set forth by the planning committee.

After reviewing the responses received, the president and provost issued a memorandum to the university community in May, 1989, that summarized for each program the subcommittee's recommendations, the college responses and the president's and provost's decisions concerning actions on major organizational and curricular issues. Many of the recommendations, as initially proposed, or as modified as a result of subsequent discussions, were identified for implementation; some were rejected; and others were designated for further study before a decision is reached. It was announced that curricular issues will be reviewed by the Faculty Senate before final action is taken and that the Board of Regents will have an opportunity to review the president's and provost's proposals. Necessary actions by these groups are expected to occur during 1990. The central administration has assured current students and those entering in Fall 1989 that they will be able to complete their chosen curricula. Tenured faculty have been assured of continuation of employment; should any faculty member's assigned responsibilities change substantially as a result of program changes, opportunities will be provided for appropriate faculty development.

VI. PROPOSALS FOR ONGOING STRATEGIC PLANNING AND PROGRAM REVIEW

The Long-Range Strategic Planning Committee recommended that strategic planning continue and become an ongoing process for the university as a whole, as well as for the various individual units of the institution. The 1987-1989 planning activities were viewed as the first phase of strategic planning, in which the appropriate focus was university-wide issues and academic programs. The committee identified the need for subsequent review of, and planning for, the significant nonacademic and key service areas of the university, including specifically the library. The committee saw ongoing strategic planning as the best process by which the university can monitor the external environment and can adapt to meet the challenges and opportunities it faces.

The planning committee made a number of specific recommendations for an ongoing planning process and structure. These recommendations called for: broad-based input; linking budget allocations to planning priorities; creation of a pool of flexible funds through internal reallocation in order to implement the plans; coordination of strategic planning by the provost; and providing appropriate staff support for planning. A detailed proposal was also made to establish, as an essential part of the ongoing strategic planning process, periodic academic program review that involves both self-study and external peer assessment. It was suggested that a comparable protocol be developed and implemented for the comprehensive and periodic review of nonacademic units and key support services. The evaluation of these areas should focus on the extent to which they provide support for the achievement of the university's mission in the interrelated areas of teaching, research and outreach. To do so, the reviews and evaluations should involve persons with academic appointments, nonacademic personnel and users of the services.

VII. RELATIONSHIP TO OTHER STUDIES

Iowa State began strategic planning in Spring 1987 with the appointment of the Long-Range Strategic Planning Committee. Following that time, several external studies were launched that were designed to examine some of the same issues but within different contexts. In Fall 1987 the State Board of Regents decided to hire a consulting firm to conduct an "organizational audit' of the Board, the Board Office and the three state universities under the Board's purview. The accounting firm of Peat Marwick was hired, at a cost of $1.25 million, to conduct the audit, which was initially scheduled to be completed by December 31, 1988. Most parts of the study were completed by the Summer of 1989, including the most controversial part which was designed to identify "potentially unnecessary" program duplication among the three Regent universities. The program duplication study examined in detail five broadly defined program areas and sparked much controversy by calling for the elimination of some large, high-quality programs at each of the three universities. The universities were given several months to respond to the recommendations, with decisions made by the Board of Regents in Fall 1989.

Several of the recommendations for Iowa State University conflicted with those that emerged from the first phase of its own strategic planning process. The university administration successfully argued that its institutional study was a more comprehensive one and that its own proposals were based upon more well-informed and well-conceived criteria, accompanied by more meaningful and relevant rationales. In the end, the Board of Regents affirmed this view. Other parts of the organizational audit directly reaffirmed some of Iowa State's strategic planning recommendations, including those for the establishment of ongoing strategic planning and the adoption of periodic academic program review.

During Spring 1988, the Iowa General Assembly approved a

two-year study of all of higher education in the state (Regents' universities, area community colleges and the state's numerous independent colleges and universities). A Higher Education Task Force (composed of seven citizens, four legislators, and a professional staff) was established to develop a 20-year plan for post-secondary education in Iowa. The report was released late in 1989. Possible changes in the state's higher education system are expected to be a major issue in the 1990 governor's election campaign.

During Summer 1988, the Governor of Iowa, the Honorable Terry E. Branstad, initiated his own study of post-secondary education in Iowa and brought together officials from all segments of higher education in the state. The Peat Marwick accounting firm was hired, at a cost of $200,000, to draft a higher education plan for Iowa. In June 1989, the Governor announced his intention to form a State Strategic Planning Council for Higher Education.

The external studies and planning efforts described above indicate the widespread interest in Iowa in examining higher education. By launching its own internal strategic planning process before the other studies were conceived and initiated, Iowa State University found itself in the strong position of being able to provide input to these external studies and to respond to proposals that emerged from them. As the president explained to the Iowa State University community, ". . . we have gained for ourselves a strategic advantage in undertaking a comprehensive self-examination before the release of the recommendations to be made by others external to the university."[2]

VIII. CONCLUSIONS

The process of strategic planning at Iowa State University was lengthy, systematic and comprehensive, but for the faculty it was also a painful and sometimes highly divisive activity that strained morale for a period of almost two years. In retrospect, the effort of the Long-Range Strategic Planning Committee represented a politically courageous and generally successful attempt on the part of its members to meet the charges assigned by the president of the university, charges necessitated by very substantial financial difficulties that had gone unresolved for too long.

The university is now in the process of reviewing and debating the last of the major recommendations offered by the committee to the campus community in the second of its major findings documents. It has emerged from the process perhaps somewhat shaken, certainly chastened, but undeniably with a new and significant sense of direction.

The faculty is now engaged here and there in discussions concerning implementation of various recommendations made by the committee, tempered and modified by campus and college debate and rational negotiation. Compromises have been made along the way, many of which improve upon the committee's original proposals.

It is perhaps worthwhile to cite an observation from the committee's first planning document, released in November 1988. It was observed that strategic planning is a "revealing" process. Perceived programmatic strengths and weaknesses were made public to the campus community and external constituents, many for the first time. Numbers of these were challenged; some were vociferously resented or vigorously rejected by those directly affected; still others were accepted or embraced with enthusiasm as essentially correct assessments of program strengths. The committee noted that such revelations, and the recommendations for change that accompanied them, both "strain" and "challenge" the institution that receives them.

Perhaps the most significant implication to emerge from this massive effort and the intense debate it engendered on campus is that the process of institutional planning is a critical and basic necessity, but one driven too often by external necessity or threatening circumstances, rather than by recognition of the fact that large organizations such as universities are living organisms that must be vigilant to continuous adjustment to the changing circumstances in which they function. Universities inherently are conservative institutions and too often they await making changes which they are forced to do by external circumstances that have taken overly long to be recognized. To do so is to court a difficult and acrimonious process. Institutional review and planning must be an ongoing activity that recognizes that the need to change is both continuous and, today, accelerating. The longer an institution delays in admitting to the need for healthy and objective self-examination and corrective prescription, the more difficult the task will be. Ours was difficult, but the institution has survived it, the attendant stress is now receding and the future is looking considerably brighter.

Obviously, it is still too early to determine the level of success of Iowa State's strategic planning. Such judgments await the passage of time and the inquiry of history, but programmatic review and strategic planning are now a permanent part of the Iowa State landscape. The findings that follow from these activities will be used to dictate the distribution of resources in the future. Budgeting will now have a rational and objective basis, as opposed to an inertial, a political, an opportunistic or a whimsical one.

NOTES

1. Edward Schuh, "Revitalizing Land Grant Universities: It's Time To Regain Relevance," *Choices* (Second Quarter 1986): 6-10.
2. Gordon P. Eaton, *Colloquium* (an occasional letter from the president to the Iowa State University Community) January 19, 1989.

Inserting the Library into a Broader Campus Planning Process

Nancy L. Eaton

SUMMARY. The execution of a planning process for a library system is not always neat and tidy, particularly if a new dean of library services enters the scene with various processes already under way and immediate problems which must be given priority. This article discusses how the ISU Library staff is trying to mesh its own internal planning process with that of the university planning and program review which has been under way for several years.

THE CONTEXT

Iowa State University of Science and Technology appointed a new Dean of Library Services on July 1, 1989. During the campus interview in March and subsequent campus visits in April and May following the appointment, the new dean was made aware by library faculty and staff of an ongoing campus planning process. It was clear that the planning process might change campus priorities significantly. The library faculty and staff expressed concern that the library was not a component of the planning process. The Provost articulated at that time that the planning process was seen as a two-part process, the first iteration to be focused on academic programs and the second iteration to include support services and non-academic units which would be impacted by changes in academic program priorities. That understanding is made clear in the Adams-Eaton article:

Nancy L. Eaton is Dean of Library Services at Iowa State University of Science and Technology at Ames, IA.

Thus, the committee recommended that the support units and nonacademic services be addressed in subsequent phases of strategic planning and become part of the ongoing process for strategic planning for Iowa State University. The library constitutes the critical and fundamental depository of most of the knowledge held and nurtured by the institution and, as such, it is a key element of the academic enterprise. In the initial strategic planning process undertaken at Iowa State, discussions and recommendations concerning the library were held in abeyance, awaiting a determination first of recommended programmatic emphasis and enhancement.[1]

Several other activities within the Regents' system or the state were under way as the new dean assumed her position on July 1, 1989, which had implications for future library priorities. The Board of Regents had requested an interinstitutional study of library cooperation among the three public institutions under its purview (University of Iowa, Iowa State University, and University of Northern Iowa); and an ad hoc committee composed of one faculty member and one librarian from each of the three campuses had been approved by the Board in November, 1988 to conduct the review of library cooperation.[2] The Iowa State Library had just concluded a statewide study of library services under the auspices of a "Blue Ribbon Panel" of librarians, citizens, and legislators.[3] That study resulted in increased funding for the state library's interlibrary lending network; and the state library subsequently proposed an "open access" program, whereby all citizens of the state would have full library privileges in any library in Iowa. Participation in the "open access" program was voluntary; and the Iowa State University Library was faced with deciding whether to participate. Finally, the Iowa Chapter of the Association of College and Research Libraries (ACRL) had been awarded a grant to hold a statewide planning retreat during the fall of 1989 to explore the need for further cooperative programs among the academic libraries of Iowa.

Within the university, a review of computation and information technology was under way. The Provost and the Vice President for Business and Finance had appointed the Computation and Information Technology Advisory Committee (CITAC) in the fall of 1988 to examine the areas of academic computing, administrative computing, and telecommunications and to develop objectives and strategies for the next three to five years to enhance computing at Iowa State University. That committee report was completed in June, 1989, and had a number of important recommendations that pertained to library automation and delivery of electronic information.[4]

Juxtaposed to these various studies or planning activities which were under way within the university or the state was the reality of the internal planning needs of the library system. While many individual studies had been conducted for specific purposes, such as a consultant's report and internal study on preservation and conservation, the library lacked any overall document indicating short-term or long-term priorities within the library. Nor had the library's budget process ever been incorporated into any broader planning process to ensure that funds were distributed in support of articulated priorities.

A more pressing problem, however, was the fact that the library's automation vendor for its online catalog had entered Chapter 11 bankruptcy proceedings for reorganization of the company's assets. Because of the uncertainty about the vendor's ability to support the system or its longterm viability as a company, planning within the library had been put on hold for almost a year. Decisions about basic operations had not been made because staff did not know what automated system they might be using in the future. Also of concern to many staff was the very decentralized structure and uncertain staffing within the library to support an expanding agenda for library automation — the current online catalog, a proliferation of microcomputers, and possible new applications such as a local area network and CD-ROM databases.

In the fall of 1989, the Board of Regents requested that Iowa State University provide it with a forecast of the resources necessary for the university to improve its national standing as a major land-grant university. Even though the library had not been part of the first iteration of the university's strategic planning process, the Provost and Dean of Library Services agreed that the library should be included in this resource projection. The report is due to the Board of Regents in April, 1990.

To complicate matters even more, the Iowa legislature approved

$50,000,000 over a five year period to implement a statewide fiber-optic communications network which would include the three Regents' institutions; and the legislation specifically included libraries in the network. Thus, there was an immediate need for the campus to begin planning for how it would participate in the network and utilize it.[5]

THE SORTING OUT PROCESS

It was the dean's judgment that the first priority was to resolve the issue of what automation system would be used by the library. Not only was the daily operation of the library at risk if the current vendor were to go out of business or fail to provide reliable maintenance; but decision-making within the library had to be freed from the vendor's uncertain future. In addition, the current system as contracted for had reached its maximum capacity, and new resources were needed to expand the library's database. Thus, evaluation of the current system as compared to other options became the first priority for the library administration. A special committee composed of library administrators, directors of the two computing centers on campus, and two faculty members from the university's Library Committee reviewed the options and recommended that the library convert from the current online catalog to the NOTIS integrated system. The university administration approved that recommendation, and a contract was signed in December of 1989. In order to facilitate the conversion from the existing system to the new system, additional consulting aid from NOTIS staff was contracted for by the library to speed up the configuration of the system and database conversion. Once the decision was made to convert to the NOTIS system and preliminary training sessions were held to familiarize staff with its design and features, the library staff was able to begin internal planning for operations once again.

The three library directors of the Regents' universities met in August, 1989, to discuss cooperation among the three Regents' libraries. The charge to the interinstitutional ad hoc committee studying cooperation among the three libraries was to "be assured that the universities are doing everything reasonable to be cost effective."[6] Because all three libraries had experienced recent changes in leadership, it appeared to the three deans/directors that credibility with the Board of Regents and assurances that the three institutions would support interinstitutional cooperation were a high priority. Thus, all three directors have devoted significant time during 1989/ 90 to the committee working on this report and to interaction with their respective academic officers and the Board staff concerning recommendations in the ad hoc committee's final report, which was submitted in November, 1989.[7] The three directors have since prepared a response to the committee's report and expect to meet further with their respective academic officers, the Board staff, and the Board of Regents concerning the committee recommendations.

The implications of the State Library's proposal for "open access" were sufficiently complex that the three Regents' library directors felt the need for a cautious approach to the program which had to include consultation with appropriate faculty committees and university administrators. The three directors continue to work with the State Librarian on the proposal's applicability to the three university libraries. The program was presented to the university's Library Committee at its January, 1990, meeting; and the committee endorsed the ISU library's cooperation in the program, conditional upon annual evaluation of its impact upon availability of materials to ISU faculty and staff. It was the Library Committee's position that the "open access" program was consistent with the university's role as a land-grant university so long as it did not have a detrimental effect upon access to library materials for the library's primary clientele. The conditions under which the ISU library will participate in the "open access" program are still being refined in conjunction with the State Librarian and should be integrated into the library's evolving set of priorities.

The state chapter ACRL planning retreat was a stimulating experience but did not result in any specific plans for statewide cooperation among academic libraries. Therefore, this activity has had little effect upon the ISU library's own plans to date.

A number of organizational responses have been made to technical issues facing the campus. First, the directors of Administrative Data Processing, the academic Computation Center, Telecommunications, the Media Resource Center, the Library, and Printing Services have begun to meet monthly to stimulate campuswide approaches to technical planning for the university. Second, a campuswide committee is being formed by the Provost to begin planning for utilization of the state's imminent fiber-optic network. Within the library, the Dean's Council has approved plans for formalizing the conservation/preservation program and for creating a Systems Office within the library to bring together the various components of library automation, to be administered by a new Assistant Director for Systems.

The most critical planning activity following selection of a new integrated system for the library, however, has been the Regents' request for a university plan to improve its standing as a nationally recognized land-grant institution. The Provost's agreement that the library is to be included in the university's response has provided a mechanism for integrating the library's planning into that of the university's planning process. All academic deans, including the Dean of Library Services, were asked to brief key university administrators on their respective college/unit needs in response to Regents' request. This provided an opportunity for library administrators to prepare a statistical profile of the library as it compares to libraries of benchmark institutions and to project several scenarios for the future, in terms of both funding and programs. This same presentation is being given to the library faculty and the university's Library Committee for purposes of background and to stimulate thinking about future priorities.

Once the Board of Regents react to the university's April planning document, ISU colleges and the library are expected to provide the Board with college-specific plans based on the university's April document and the university's stratetgic planning process. The projected due date for the college-specific plans is November, 1990. The library administration has chosen to use this as a target date for completing a five-year plan for the library system which would be updated annually in conjunction with the university's final methodology for a continuing strategic planning process and would be tied to budget requests and allocations.

PROCESS TO BE USED BY THE LIBRARY

The report of the Long-Range Strategic Planning Committee is specific about the process it recommends for support units to be integrated into the university's strategic planning process:

> While the Long-Range Strategic Planning Committee did not develop a detailed protocol for the review of non-academic and support services, the committee recommends that such a protocol be developed and implemented, consistent with the following general guidelines. The review of the nonacademic areas and services should be as comparable as is appropriate to the proposed review of academic programs in terms of: the degree of comprehensiveness of the reviews; the periodic nature of the reviews; the development of adequate data bases for evaluation; the responsibility for coordination and staff support; and the combination of internal self-study followed by external review. The evaluation of nonacademic areas and services should focus on the extent to which they provide support for the achievement of the university's mission in the interrelated areas of teaching, research, and outreach. To do so, the reviews and evaluations should involve persons with academic appointments, nonacademic personnel, and users of the services.[8]

It is the intent of the library administration that Dean's Council, which includes all department heads and assistant directors within the library plus the president of the Library Staff Association, and the university's Library Committee will be key components in the planning process. Department heads will work with their respective departments in drafting departmental input to the planning process. Those groups do not include student representation or constituencies outside the university, however; and those constituencies must also be included in the planning process. The mechanics of how that input will be solicited are yet to be determined. An Associate Provost was appointed as of January 1, 1990 to facilitate the campus planning process; and the library administration has already made contact with that individual for purposes of meshing the library's efforts with the university's ongoing process.

KEY ELEMENTS IN THE LIBRARY STRATEGIC PLANNING PROCESS

The various planning documents under way when the Dean of Library Services arrived on July 1, 1989, provide input into the environmental scan of issues facing allocation of library resources in the future. These include but are not limited to the following:

1. Changing emphasis in the university's programs which would necessitate changes in program support from the library's materials and access budget. The university's planning report identified five areas of enhanced scholarly emphasis which might effect the library's distribution of resources.[9]
2. New technologies to be adapted by the library, such as the integrated library system, indexing/abstracting data bases mounted on local mainframes, telecommunications networks (the campus ISN network; the state fiber-optic network; the OCLC national network; commercial networks; and an in-house local area network); and CD-ROM technology.
3. Organizational structure within the library needed to support programs, staff training, supervision, etc.
4. Cooperative efforts—intrastate and interstate.
5. Responsibilies for outreach activities such as a land-grant library.
6. Funds, staffing and facilities needed to support programs and collection; possible reallocation of resources to meet a portion of those resources needed; and possible outside resources available (i.e., grants, federal funds, capital campaign donors, etc.)

CONCLUSION

The new Dean of Library Services was greeted by a panoply of studies, planning processes, and assumptions about the library's role in the future of the university and state and about its resource needs. Within the first six months, however, a methodology has emerged which will allow the library to become integrated into the campus planning process. Given the variety of expectations abounding, even an imperfect first generation planning document which is to be produced by November, 1990, will be a vast improvement over the current situation; and the expectation is that the planning document would be updated each year and tied to budget requests and allocations.

NOTES

1. Adams, Jean W. and Eaton, Gordon P. "Strategic Planning at Iowa State University: Affirmation and Expectation," *Journal of Library Administration 13 (1990)*.

2. Memorandum from Robert J. Barak and R. Wayne Richey to the Board of Regents, December 6, 1988. 2p.

3. State Library of Iowa. *New Era for Libraries*. A Report From the Iowa Blue Ribbon Task Force on Libraries. January, 1989. 18p.

4. Iowa State University. *Report of the Computation and Information Technology Advisory Committee (CITAC)*. June, 1989. [Unpublished report].

5. State of Iowa. House File 774 (1989), pp. 39-46.

6. Barak and Richey.

7. *Library Cooperation: Cooperative Efforts Among U.S. Research Libraries and Iowa Regents' Libraries*. A Study Commissioned by the State of Iowa Board of Regents. November 9, 1989. [Unpublished report].

8. *Affirmation and Expectations for Iowa's Land-Grant University*. Report of the Long-Range Strategic Planning Committee. November, 1988. p. 99. [Unpublished report].

9. Adams and Eaton.

The Dreams of the Reasonable: Integrating Library and University Planning

Jinnie Y. Davis
Karen P. Helm

SUMMARY. At North Carolina State University, a biennial planning process integrates the plans of all academic and administrative units on campus, including the Libraries. Further, the biennial planning cycle has been coordinated with the budgeting process, so budget requests must be tied directly to priorities stated in unit plans. This paper describes the incentives for instituting university planning and how it was implemented during its first cycle and improved during the second, with particular emphasis on library planning. The authors recommend linking planning to an existing decision-making process, cultivating good relationships and close communications between the university and the library levels, maintaining a proper perspective on planning, and using the plan for education and promotion.

Plans are the dreams of the reasonable.

—Feuchtersleben

INTRODUCTION

At North Carolina State University (NCSU), a biennial campus-wide planning process forms a rational framework through which dreams can become a reality. Planning at the NCSU Libraries is integrated into this process. This paper explains the incentives for

Jinnie Y. Davis is Assistant Director for Planning and Development, North Carolina State University Libraries, Raleigh, NC. Karen P. Helm is Director of University Planning at North Carolina State University, Raleigh, NC.

instituting university planning and how the process was first implemented, with a focus on planning within the library system. It also examines the effect of biennial planning on organizational behavior, both within the Libraries and at the university level. The authors report improvements in the process and conclude with recommendations for the successful integration of planning between the university and the library.

INCENTIVES FOR UNIVERSITY-LEVEL PLANNING

In the early to mid-1980s, North Carolina State University, a public research university with an enrollment of 26,000, was coping with a number of significant changes that had taken place during a few years' time and that created many incentives for more formal planning across the institution. Among these changes were: a dramatic expansion of research activity that led to a tripling of research expenditures; a shift in enrollment toward a very small number of engineering and business programs; an almost 300 percent increase in funding; and anticipation of a drastic downturn in state funding to public higher education resulting from a slowing economy and competing state priorities.

Without a rational planning process, decisions had been made on the basis of instinct rather than on the basis of clear direction and orderly progression of decisions. Although a few colleges and administrative units had developed their own plans, there was no institution-wide planning process. The only comprehensive vehicle for goal setting was budget development, which was fractured into five different processes running on different calendars and controlled by different vice chancellors. At no time were the budgets evaluated simultaneously to determine whether they were well coordinated or consistent with university goals. Without planning, budget—not academic strategies—tended to drive decisions.

IMPLEMENTING THE PLANNING PROCESS

In an effort to respond to expanding and shifting needs, and to provide more rational coordination to decisions generally and to resource allocation specifically, the chancellor asked for a planning process through which the university and each of its parts would identify and negotiate long range goals and shorter-range objectives. In addition, he wanted planning to complement the budget process, so that program goals would drive budgets, rather than vice versa. Further, to ensure that all budgets were developed in accordance with planned and negotiated goals, better coordination was needed among the five separate budget processes.

A new, two-year planning process was implemented during the 1986-87 academic year. It was designed primarily as a communication device and as a pre-budgeting negotiation of program goals. Planning documents traveled from the bottom of the institution to the top and back down again, and programs and resource needs would be negotiated at each step. Documents were kept brief (two and three pages) and written largely in "bullet" form to focus attention on the most important aspects of the plans. Because the intended product of planning was to be communication and not formal documents, the plans were not revised as a result of any negotiation, and they assumed the appearance of informal worksheets rather than finished publications.

During the first year of the cycle, university-wide long-range goals were reviewed and revised. The University Planning Committee (UPC), a largely faculty committee with limited administrative, student, and alumni representation, was asked by the chancellor to recommend long-range goals that would provide a university-wide framework for unit planning and budgeting across the university.

The UPC tapped eight task forces to study different areas of university operation and to suggest goals: academic and institutional support services, extension and public service, undergraduate instruction, research and graduate education, student support services, financial support, enrollment projections, and emerging issues. The first two task forces included representatives from the Libraries. The last task force represented the UPC's "environmental scanning" group, which looked at social, political, technological and other environmental trends and events that would likely shape NCSU's future. The task force reports were merged into a single set of recommendations that were amended, approved, and published as official "University Long-Range Goals" by the chancellor.

To initiate the second year of the biennial planning cycle, the chancellor issued the call for plans and distributed a *Planning Handbook* that included the "University Long-Range Goals," mission statement, institutional trends data, and a description of the planning and budgeting processes. Planning formats required a statement of long-range goals, biennial objectives, strategies and resources for achieving those objectives, and identification of source of funding, if required. To support this more intensive planning activity, an Office of University Planning was created with a director who would provide coordination and technical assistance to participating units.

Both academic and administrative units took part in biennial planning. Each was free to employ its own planning process, whether by involving committees, conducting a retreat, or issuing a plan by administrative fiat. Because some units already had a planning process in place, the format was intentionally brief to permit those units simply to highlight their results. Within four months of the chancellor's call for plans, academic department plans, college summary plans, administrative unit plans and division summary plans were forwarded to the Office of University Planning for review and analysis.

The Director of University Planning conducted simple analyses in an effort to assist the university administration in generating feedback to the goals and objectives in the plans. For example, summaries of new programs, new facilities, planned enrollment increases, new research centers, and other initiatives were helpful in determining whether the university as a collective had enough or too many initiatives on its wish list. These summaries also offered guidance on which initiatives would be most welcomed during subsequent budget development. The analysis of intended funding sources was helpful in giving guidance to units regarding the feasibility of their budget intentions. An analysis of congruence between the plans and the university's goals facilitated review of unit priorities.

The chancellor, provost, and vice chancellor for research provided written responses to each of the deans regarding the college plans. Vice chancellors scheduled appointments for oral discussion of plans. In all cases, the feedback was very specific about the program objectives intended for initiation and funding during the next budget cycle. This phase was concluded at the same time that the Budget Office mailed the call for budget requests.

Several reforms were made in the budget process to complement biennial planning. Four of the five primary budget processes were pulled into the same calendar, starting and finishing at the same time. Instead of holding separate hearings for each budget, a single hearing was held, which allowed the university to assess requests for operating funds, facilities, positions, new programs, and indirect cost funds as a package. Further, each request was cross-referenced to an objective in the biennial plans, and deans and vice chancellors were required to justify all requests on the basis of planned goals.

PLANNING WITHIN THE LIBRARIES

The NCSU Libraries, an organization of more than 200 employees, constitutes one of the largest participating units within the university; it reports to the provost. In 1985, the Libraries created a half-time position of Assistant to the Director for Planning (later expanded to "Planning and Development"), a librarian whose responsibilities included long-range planning within the library system. The Libraries' only major planning document, however, had just been compiled in 1985 independently of planning at other administrative levels of the university. While it was distributed across campus, there was no forum outside the library for consideration of its concerns or recommendations. With the implementation of the university-wide planning process, the Libraries discontinued its previous mode of planning via a committee and task forces. Instead, the Assistant to the Director coordinated planning according to the university's format guidelines across the main library and its five branches. The Libraries welcomed a process that would encompass the entire campus—thus ensuring that its plan would be integrated into that of the institution as a whole—and considered the correlation of plans with budget requests a logical step in enhancing the effectiveness of the institution.

Because the university imposed no uniform process for planning, the Libraries worked out its own methods. The description of the libraries' process is grouped around the issues of how the library was treated within the university; how the Libraries' plan was created; and what the limitations as to time, logistics, and format were.

(1) Treatment of the library within the university. The university suggested different planning formats of two pages for academic departments and administrative units, and three pages for colleges and administrative divisions. The Libraries was considered an administrative unit, which placed it among the ranks of offices such as Financial Aid. How could the library fit the complexity of its organization into a single unit plan? The Libraries overcame the format limitation by suggesting to the Director of University Planning that it be allowed to submit plans at two levels: four "administrative unit" level plans for the functional areas of administrative services, collection management, public services, and technical services; and a "college or division" level plan that summarized the library system's overall priorities. Approval of this expansion allowed the Libraries to cover more adequately the intricacies of its operation. The continued perception of the Libraries as an administrative unit rather than as a unit on the academic side, however, had ramifications upon the follow-up treatment of its plans. While colleges within the university received written responses from the chancellor on their plans, administrative units did not. The Libraries did receive an oral response, however, through the provost.

(2) Creation of the Libraries' plan. Should the library use a "top-down" or "bottom-up" approach to planning? Its previous long-range plan was the result of an intensive bottom-up process, whereby numerous task forces made up of professionals and support staff studied issues that were compiled into reports which were then presented to the Director of Libraries, along with an overall planning report. This time, there was a planning librarian on the staff as well as a newly formed Directors Council (composed of the director and three assistant directors), advisory to a new Director of Libraries. The library administration decided that the Assistant to the Director for Planning and Development would coordinate and lead initial planning meetings of appropriate staff members—primarily assistant directors and department heads—for each of the four functional areas. At these meetings, the groups, in consultation with staff members in their departments, developed statements of long-range goals and lists in priority order of objectives, related to the goals, to be met during the period of 1988-1991. They also

ranked probable objectives for subsequent biennia in order of importance. Next the staff delineated specific strategies to accomplish the stated objectives.

During this process, there was frequent exchange of information between the library's planning officer and members of the Directors Council. As the plans unfolded, they underwent multiple revisions as each iteration strived for clarity and succinctness. Then the Directors Council assigned to each strategy a designation of its expected funding sources. Following categories established by the Office of University Planning, the council indicated whether accomplishment of each strategy would come from: (A) reallocations within the library, (B) new allocations of state funds to the library, (C) other sources (e.g., contracts, grants, development funds), or (D) if no new resources were required. This categorization proved to be of use to the Libraries' later development efforts, when it was able to draw upon a list of all items designated as category "C" in the biennial plan as potential fund-raising projects.

The director, in consultation with the Directors Council and the planning officer, then compiled the overall, school-level plan. As a summary that would have broad distribution across campus, this plan emphasized the NCSU Libraries' long-range goals in the context of the university's programs. It selected the most crucial objectives from the four unit plans, noted the priority assigned to each at the unit level, and arranged them in a new order of priority from the perspective of the library system as a whole.

(3) Limitations of time, logistics, and format. Unlike NCSU's colleges, the library as an administrative unit only had one and a half (instead of two and a half) months to complete its portion of the plan. The desire to include library staff at all levels in the planning process meant that departmental meetings, divisional meetings, and Directors Council meetings all had to be scheduled within a short space of time. Use of a fairly rigid word processing program with limited microcomputer access also hindered the process of compiling the final report. Another limitation was the university's enjoiner to begin each statement of objective with one of the four words "sustain," "establish," "enhance," or "expand." This restriction led to certain convolutions in phrasing, to cover activities that would be reduced or projects that would be completed during the biennium.

OUTCOMES OF BIENNIAL PLANNING
FOR ORGANIZATIONAL BEHAVIOR

At the university level, the most important outcome was the shift in focus of the budgeting and resource allocation process toward planned program goals. For the first time, discussion during budget hearings focused more on what colleges and administrative divisions were trying to achieve programmatically than on bottom-line cost. Even discussions of cost moved dramatically away from line-item detail toward much larger increments of cost and, thus, toward a larger perspective of the university than had been evident previously. The insistence that all budget requests be cross-referenced to biennial plans provided a very strong incentive for all participants to take planning very seriously and ensure that the documents accurately reflect their goals and objectives. Further, the requirement that participants identify funding sources during the planning phase helped them to coordinate all five budgets.

For many units on campus, biennial planning was their first planning effort. For the first time, faculty and administrators were asked to identify as a group the unit's long-range directions and its shorter-range priorities. Many participants reported that the planning exercise helped them to understand how decisions were made on campus and how to become more competitive for limited resources.

These behavioral shifts were reflected in the NCSU Libraries. The practical applications of its biennial plan over the next two years reinforced for its staff the library's stated priorities. Whenever internal decisions on allocation of resources had to be made, library departments and divisions were asked to reference their requests—whether for personnel, equipment, or supplies—to the goal or objective supported in the biennial plan. The library administration ensured that its budget requests to the university administration were directly tied to the top goals of its plan. The plan thus served to aid administrative decision making by the Directors Council.

The integration of the library into the university-wide process helped to give the Libraries' goals more prominence among the university administrators. Because the Director of Libraries reports to the provost, the library's biennial plan went to the provost's office, where it was reduced and recast into another summary form, listing an overall order of priority for all units under the purview of the provost. In addition, a summary of the Libraries' plan was published, along with all other unit plans, in the campus-wide *Official Bulletin*.

Another critical outcome was the installation of the biennial plan as a focal point for publicizing priorities among library activities. A copy of the plan was sent to every library staff member. The plan was also incorporated into promotional aspects of the library. For example, articles on the planning process and the biennial plan appeared in the Libraries' quarterly newsletter. The Libraries also regularly sends the plan to all interviewees for professional positions. Finally, at a pivotal juncture in the library's history, the biennial plan served to establish, between the new library director and members of the library staff, a set of mutually agreed-upon goals, objectives, and strategies by which to chart a course into the future.

CONTINUING TO DEVELOP
THE PLANNING PROCESS

As the second planning cycle began in 1988, several improvements were made on the basis of experience and a series of follow-up interviews with deans, department heads, vice chancellors, the UPC, provost, and chancellor. First, the "University Long-Range Goals," which are developed during the first year of planning, received much more attention than they had during the first cycle. Because they were used as decision-making principles, the UPC took greater care in soliciting faculty, staff and student reactions to drafts before making recommendations to the chancellor. Further, the chancellor asked that the Deans Council approve the goals as a way of validating and making official what a faculty committee had recommended.

Second, the planning process began three months earlier to allow units that host summer retreats to focus some of their retreat agenda on goals and priorities, and to facilitate better faculty involvement at the department level. Third, the feedback phase was expanded. Instead of communicating only through the written medium, which could be easily misinterpreted, the chancellor invited each dean and vice chancellor to a meeting to review the plans and to negotiate feedback face-to-face.

The most significant change to the university's planning process came about as a result of new institutional accreditation criteria calling for regular planning and evaluation processes to assess institutional effectiveness. This change required that the process be viewed not simply as a pre-budgeting exercise, but also as the vehicle through which the institution and each of its parts would report on progress toward program goals and needed changes identified as a result of program evaluation. These requirements were met by adding new elements to the planning format: a mission statement, progress report on goals stated in the previous plan, and measures for each long-range goal.

The Libraries' Assistant to the Director for Planning and Development was among those who responded to the Director of University Planning's request for comments on the first cycle. Thus several of the library's suggestions for changes were incorporated into the second cycle, when minor inconveniences like the restrictions on wording were removed. A way was also found around a more substantive limitation. The Libraries and NCSU Academic Computing had been cooperating increasingly on several projects. There was no easy way, however, to call attention to the cooperative nature of these joint goals and objectives. At the suggestion of the Director of University Planning, the Libraries and Academic Computing compiled a joint biennial plan in addition to the separate biennial plan for each unit. The goals and objectives of this collaborative plan were cross-referenced to pertinent items in the individual plans and covered such combined efforts as the establishment of a joint research and instructional facility for computation and information management. The joint plan helped the university administration evaluate the institution-wide funding needs associated with one of its most important long-range goals: ensuring full development of the "electronic infrastructure," including all computing and information systems.

Lessons learned within the Libraries from the first cycle were also applied to the second planning cycle. The previous use of four unit-level plans and one college-level plan had helped the library staff to lay out its goals within a familiar framework of traditional functions during a time of transition to new goals and objectives. In actual use, however, the multitude of plans and levels caused some confusion as well. In addition, the breakdown into four units meant that goals crossing divisional lines had to be repeated under each unit. In the second cycle, the Libraries submitted a single, integrated biennial plan that was still able to cover all library functions.

The Libraries also took a more active role in determining exactly how the Office of University Planning evaluated each plan. Not only was the University's *Planning Handbook* distributed to each assistant director in the library, but the Libraries' planning officer invited the Director of University Planning to speak at a meeting of library department heads on the planning process and environmental factors affecting the next planning cycle. The Director of University Planning also attended a Directors Council meeting to explain how each plan was analyzed. For example, a key factor was pertinence to the university's stated goals and objectives; the Libraries revised the wording of its goals accordingly, as well as to ensure the avoidance of library jargon and a narrow library perspective. Where a goal might originally have been phrased as "Expand and enhance efforts to continue development of an online integrated library system," after review it was changed to "Enhance the online integrated library system's capability to meet NCSU's information and research needs." Needs for resources were never expressed as ends in themselves, but always tied to a goal ultimately related to a university-level goal (e.g., not "Add more library staff" but "Add four library staff to meet the expanding academic and research needs of the Centennial Campus").

In the planning process itself, the Assistant to the Director for Planning and Development's role shifted to that of a coordinator and compiler, with less time spent in attending meetings. With an existing biennial plan to build upon and with top library administrators who had gained experience from the last cycle, the assistant directors took on the majority of the planning sessions on goals, objectives and strategies with their staff. While this portion of the process was accelerated, time required to complete the new elements during the second cycle — mission statement, progress report, and measures of progress — added to the length of the schedule.

The library used several additional techniques to vary the involvement of its staff in planning. To obtain a draft of the progress made on the previous goals, small-group discussions were held at a department heads' meeting. Each group discussed a functional area to assess progress made so far, and one group considered environmental factors that would have an impact on the next biennial plan. Asking library staff to participate in these discussions helped to spread an awareness of just how far the library had come in achieving the objectives of its first biennial plan. The Libraries also held its first all day planning retreat for all department heads and assistant directors. Generating ideas on measures of progress for the goals of the second plan was part of the agenda and formed the draft of that section of the planning document.

Thus different groups held concurrent meetings at all levels to create drafts of the major portions of the plan, which the Assistant to the Director for Planning and Development combined into the correct format for review and modification by the Directors Council. The draft was then discussed at the department heads' retreat, and revised and reviewed again by the Directors Council. Also simultaneously, the Assistant Director for Library Systems oversaw the production of the Libraries' collaborative plan with Academic Computing. Both plans were subsequently distributed to all members of the library staff, and the Director of Libraries held two full-staff meetings to discuss and answer questions about the two plans.

During this cycle, the library staff was able to make the wording of goals and of objectives more consistent than in the first plan, resisting the temptation to retain objectives or strategies that were of relatively minor importance. Library planners also found it easier to accept the idea of a shorter, less detailed plan as one that would not only make more of an impact among university administrators but also be easier for library staff members themselves to refer to and remember. Because the plans project activities for up to four years in the future, describing goals in broad strokes also allowed the library more flexibility in means to achieve them, especially in areas where external factors (e.g., new technologies) fluctuate rapidly.

The improvement of word processing capabilities at the Libraries since the first cycle also contributed immensely to successful logistics. The Libraries had increased its microcomputer workstations to forty and had linked them into a local area network with an electronic mail feature. The resulting improvement in communications and the ready availability of more powerful word processing programs were of tremendous help in generating all stages of the draft and producing a more attractive final document.

The planning process must continue to be a flexible, evolutionary one. The next cycle will undergo further modification, based on the experiences of the second cycle and in response to pertinent external factors at the time.

RECOMMENDATIONS FOR SUCCESSFUL PLANNING AND INTEGRATION BETWEEN UNIVERSITY AND LIBRARY PLANNING

As is often the case, recommendations about a process after one has experienced it seem often to be merely applications of common sense. For those libraries that have not undergone a university-wide planning process, however, the following may be of help.

(1) Tie planning directly to an existing decision-making process. At NCSU, this tie was accomplished through the university's insistence that the priorities of the planning documents be the basis according to which budgetary resources are allocated. The Libraries instituted similar references between the plan and resource allocation to prevent the plan from becoming another document that merely gathers dust on a shelf.

(2) Cultivate good relationships and close communications between the university administration and the library administration, including their planning officers. Planning processes are merely tools to achieve an end and should not be ends in themselves. Receptivity to change and flexibility within general uniformity can go far in smoothing this process. At both the university and the library level, it is useful to have a professional with responsibility for the coordination of planning, as well as to serve as a resource person and liaison. Further, both planning officers should solicit the advice of administrators in designing and improving the planning process, because only those individuals fully understand the nuts and bolts of planning and its effective implementation at the unit level.

(3) Maintain a proper perspective on planning. Although li-

braries will need internal documents that can specify the fine points of "cleaning up dirty MARC records," this degree of detail in this jargon is unnecessary to present to the university. Remember that the university administrators you wish most to influence will be faced with reading hundreds of pages of other plans as well. A minimum of brief but understandable statements that are relevant to stated university priorities will be likely to make more of an impression.

(4) Use the plan for education and promotion. Library plans that will be distributed across the campus as part of an overall document can offer a chance to educate university administrators and faculty about the purpose and potential of an academic research library. Where NCSU's library planners violated their rule of brevity, it was to ensure that a non-library public would understand the statement. A collection management strategy, for example, attempts to educate the uninformed reader as well: "Expand resources for collections to a level adequate for responding to demands of current and emerging research and teaching programs by (a) building in strategies to cope with uncertain budgets, inflationary and market trends in publishing, and currency fluctuations; (b) increasing materials budget to regain lost purchasing power and to support new and emerging programs; and (c) developing a new allocation model supported by a budget management and information system."

Because the library's plan will also project to its readers an image of the organization, the NCSU Libraries staff tried to express ideas without lapsing into the familiar or trite. Where its 1985 mission statement began "To acquire, organize, and preserve recorded knowledge and information . . .," the 1989 one begins with: "To be on the leading edge of information services, access, and delivery" and ends with: "To pursue excellence in all our endeavors."

ATTAIN THE DREAMS OF THE REASONABLE

In the Libraries' assessment of its progress so far on the first plan for the period from 1988 to 1991 (the evaluation was conducted in fall of 1989), the staff determined that progress had indeed been made on every goal. An analysis of the planned strategies shows that, halfway into the planning period, 84 percent have already been addressed (36 percent of the stated strategies have been carried out, and 48 percent are in progress). Only 16 percent remain to be addressed, and many of them are subsequent stages of the strategies in progress. The integrated planning process has indeed aided the library in formulating its goals and channelling its resources to attain its highest priorities. For the university as a whole, biennial planning has proven itself as a valuable tool in shaping institutional budgets and decisions according to a shared vision and rationally developed priorities.

REFERENCES

North Carolina State University. Office of University Planning. "Planning handbook, 1989." North Carolina State University, Office of University Planning, Raleigh. Photocopy.

North Carolina State University Computing Center and North Carolina State University Libraries. "Collaborative Biennial Plan, 1991-1993: Computing Center and the NCSU Libraries." North Carolina State University, The Libraries, Raleigh. Photocopy.

North Carolina State University Libraries. "[Biennial plan, 1988-1991] . . . November 16, 1987." North Carolina State University, The Libraries, Raleigh. Photocopy.

North Carolina State University Libraries. "NCSU Libraries — Biennial Plan, 1991-1993, November 3, 1989." North Carolina State University, The Libraries, Raleigh. Photocopy.

Refocusing, Rebalancing, and Refining (R³): The Libraries' Role in Strategic Long-Range Planning at Michigan State University

Beth J. Shapiro

SUMMARY. At Michigan State University, long-range planning has existed for many years. Its current planning effort, Refocusing, Rebalancing, and Refining (R³) has been implemented effectively within the University Libraries with significant benefits. First, the staff became better informed about library funding which resulted in better and more realistic program proposals. Second, the staff are moving more effectively into the strategic planning process being implemented by the new director. Third, R³ has provided the Libraries with an effective platform from which to emphasize with University administrators the important role played by the Libraries in all academic enterprises. And finally, staff participation in the process provided them with a real sense of empowerment.

During the last thirty years, many institutions have implemented program budgeting, long-range planning structures, and/or strategic planning both to establish organizational priorities and to allocate resources more effectively in response to increased demands coupled with limited resources.

At Michigan State University (MSU), long-range planning is not a new phenomenon, surfacing in various forms in each of the last

---

Beth J. Shapiro is Deputy Director of the Michigan State University Libraries, East Lansing, MI.

four decades. The University Libraries, as an academic unit, has been represented in many, but not all, of these endeavors and has participated annually in the program planning review process, but has not played a significant role in the actual development of campus planning procedures.

At the present time, the University is engaged in a process that blends aspects of both long-range and strategic planning. "Refocusing, Rebalancing, and Refining," more commonly known as "R³," contains multi-year planning horizons, which is typical of a long-range planning process, yet also provides for the high visibility and prominence of external environmental tendencies affecting all of higher education and a strong component of faculty and staff participation, which is characteristic of strategic planning processes.[1]

This paper will describe the tradition of long-range planning at MSU, the current strategic long-range planning program, and the role and impact of these planning activities on the University Libraries and its staff.

PLANNING WITHIN THE UNIVERSITY PRIOR TO R³

In 1959, John Hannah, President of Michigan State University, appointed a Committee on the Future of the University. At that time, the University was growing rapidly and this committee was established to identify institutional priorities and to develop a plan of action for addressing future demands on the university. This was a highly centralized planning effort involving a relatively small number of people.

The Report to the President from the Committee on the Future of the University (1959) stressed the need for the University to be devoted to excellence while being selective in its emphasis. In addition to dealing with issues such as undergraduate and graduate education, research facilities and resources, off-campus programs, student services, faculty recruitment and support, and public relations, the Committee's work addressed the current state of long-range planning at the University and developed recommendations to institutionalize planning for the future.

The Committee proposed establishing generally understood criteria to determine whether a specific program is central, peripheral, or detrimental to the mission of the University; establishing a flow of information to facilitate the assessment of programs based on these criteria; that each department and college prepare long-range plans consistent with the objectives and mission established for the University; and, that these plans be reviewed by appropriate educational and policy groups. In addition, it was proposed that these plans be submitted to the legislature and be made available for public review at budget request time (Committee on the Future of the University 1959, 62-63).

The Director of Libraries was a member of the Committee on the Future of the University and many recommendations concerning the Library were reflected throughout the report. Library facilities and resources were so inadequate in 1959, that the Director surmised that the issue of improving library facilities, collections, and services was of such importance to the faculty, that the Library would have received attention even if he had not been a member of the Committee (telephone interview with Richard E. Chapin, 6 February 1990).

While some of the long-range planning proposals were not implemented as described, special focus task forces and committees were appointed from 1967-1973 to address several of the issues identified in the 1959 report as requiring additional review (Long Range Planning Council 1978, 1).

By 1973, a standardized Annual Evaluation and Report (AER) procedure was implemented to systematize the preparation of the University's annual budget request to the legislature. Subsequently, this was replaced by the All Funds Program and Budget Planning Report. Both planning procedures were initiated by central university administration. The unit plans moved through the colleges to central administration and were used as a basis for resource allocation and program decisions. Since the University Libraries was considered an academic unit, rather than a support service unit, the University Libraries was required to submit these documents. Typically they were prepared by the Director without input from staff or any users.

In 1975, the President of the University stated that prevailing economic conditions in the State required the initiation of a long-range planning effort within the university in order to better allocate limited resources. For FY77, the AER was revised to redirect units away from focusing on the past and towards the demands of the future. Shortly thereafter, the president released a report establishing planning guidelines and calling for a major reevaluation of all university operations to identify priority programs.

A Long Range Planning Council was appointed in the spring of 1977 to receive, analyze, and recommend suggestions that could not be introduced easily within existing university channels: cross-departmental issues, cross-college issues, all university concerns in order to improve both the efficiency and effectiveness of the university. The Council recommended that the university's long-range planning capability be reviewed regularly and a profile of capability attributes was outlined (Long Range Planning Council 1978, 5).

By the early 1980's, MSU's long-range strategic planning process was beginning to take form. Central planning documents consisted of six related documents providing guiding statements for long-range and strategic planning:

- Long Range Strategic Planning at Michigan State University
- Mission Statement
- Environmental Assumptions
- University Goals
- Academic Programs: Michigan State University
- Support Service Programs: Michigan State University

As described in the "Statement of Long Range Strategic Planning at Michigan State University," the planning process was to be flexible, responsive, and ongoing with a planning horizon of three- to five-year rolling cycles with a programmatic focus (Michigan State University 1984, 2-3). The annual planning documents used by the academic and support service units have been revised throughout the 1980's and have been incorporated into the current process.

Separate planning documents exist for academic and support service units:

- Academic Program Planning and Review (APPR)
- Support Services Program Planning and Review (SSPPR)

Detailed planning, which occurs at both the major administrative unit and unit levels, requires definition of the unit's objectives and means of achieving them, analysis of the program's effectiveness, assessment of alternatives for making improvements, and projections for future plans.

> Program planning should also be based on realistic long-range budget, enrollment, and facility projections, and other appropriate planning assumptions. (Michigan State University 1984, 8)

This process evolved at a time when the State of Michigan was faced with declining revenues. During the early 1980's, the Governor issued Executive Orders recalling previously appropriated funds in order to balance the State's budget and throughout the entire decade, State appropriations could not sustain both inflation, increased faculty salaries, and new program initiatives, such as significant investment in the technological infrastructure. In addition, the University faced considerable public pressure to keep tuition increases at or below inflation. As in the past, the Director of Libraries was required to submit an APPR for the Libraries, yet few staff, including most members of the Libraries' senior administrative staff, were involved in any real way with the process.

PLANNING WITHIN THE LIBRARIES PRIOR TO R[3]

Since a significant portion of the Report of the Committee on the Future of the University focused on the Libraries, that report became the key blueprint for action for the Libraries throughout the 1960's and 1970's. Until 1984, the Libraries had not been engaged in a planning effort separate from that of the university nor had the staff participated in any planning activities.

In the late 1970's the Libraries implemented a performance-based evaluation system for librarians. Similar to a traditional management-by-objectives system found in corporate settings, this process required an annual planning process within all units at all levels to develop annual Libraries, departmental, and unit goals and objectives to serve as an institutional framework within which personal goals and objectives were developed (Michigan State University Libraries 1979). The Libraries' annual goals and objectives statement was incorporated into the APPR beginning with 1984.

Due to the enormous transformation of the campus since the late 1950's and the dramatic changes in access to information, the Director of Libraries initiated an Association of Research Libraries (ARL) self-study planning process in 1983 to focus on the Libraries' public services program. The end product of this effort, which involved nearly a third of the staff over a ten month period, was a long-range plan for reconfiguring library services and the main library facility (Michigan State University Libraries 1983). From 1984 through 1989, most of the recommendations, or modified versions of the recommendations, in the Report of the Public Services Study Team were implemented.

Subsequently, building upon the experiences gained through the Public Services Study, several ad hoc task forces have been appointed during the last several years that have utilized a self-study approach to address specific issues or problem areas that were not addressed during the Public Services Study, such as database searching services, access to machine readable data files, review of branch libraries and unaffiliated reading rooms, and access to medical information.

REFOCUSING, REBALANCING, AND REFINING (R^3)

As a mechanism for positioning the University to more effectively meet the challenges of the decade of the 1990's, the President and Provost placed the University's planning procedures within a new framework.

The University has embarked on a new concentrated effort to assure that it is 'doing the right things, doing things right, at the right time in our history.' We call this process 'Refocusing, Rebalancing, and Refining (R³).' The task is far more than a quantitative budget-balancing exercise. It is an attempt to address intentionally the changes exerting powerful influences on the future of this University. It is also a resolve to position ourselves strategically to explore and evaluate new opportunities against the concept of a redesigned base. (Michigan State University 1989a, 1)

The process of refocusing, rebalancing, and refining must generate a creative and innovative reconfiguration of our academic culture to ensure a University that is refocused in terms of priorities, rebalanced in consideration of the equilibrium between and among academic programs, and refined to create a more effective and efficient academic enterprise. (Michigan State University 1989a, 10)

A significant change with R³ is a focus on all aspects and units of the University including a reconsideration of the University's goals and environmental assumptions to develop an appropriate "strategic vision" to guide MSU into the twenty-first century (Michigan State University 1989a, iii, 13).

Through early meetings with deans, faculty and students, a set of principles were identified to guide the process:

Thus, we shall plan in the context of our ethos — the guiding principles of our academic enterprise. Our discussions to date with members of the University community have identified as values a University that is multidimensionally excellent; multidisciplinary, built on excellent and strong departments and schools; strongly coupled, internally and externally; integrated; humanitarian, caring; built on current and selectively developed strengths; more efficient and effective; pluralistic and diverse; and has a learning environment built on new technologies. All of these values assume a certain flexibility, a willingness to risk, a sharing of agendas, and the involvement and empowerment of members of our various constituencies in shaping Michigan State University. (Michigan State University 1989a, 9)

In addition to the traditional unit reviews accomplished through the APPR process, which has been incorporated into R^3 as the key decentralized planning piece, this process is built upon five "platforms" that utilize a self-study framework. The goal of the five platforms is to develop a strategic central vision of the University as it moves towards the twenty-first century. The Libraries staff have not been key players in determining this vision although it appears as if they will be key players in the implementation phase.

Two of the planning platforms were engaged prior to the implementation of the R^3 process. A brief discussion of the five platforms and their relationship to R^3 is shown in Figure 1.

PLUS (Planning for a Lifelong University System) was begun during the 1986/87 fiscal year and resulted in a restructuring of lifelong education programs within the University. This initiative was handled as a self-study process within the Lifelong Education Programs (LEP). No Library staff members were involved with the PLUS initiative except for the Director who responded to the LEP plan as a member of the Council of Deans. Since the redesign of lifelong education programs, lifelong education issues have been addressed in the Libraries' annual planning documents though no separate planning focus within the Libraries has addressed lifelong education issues.

CRUE (Council to Review Undergraduate Education), consisted of a committee of thirty-four faculty and graduate students representing all colleges and the academic governance system. While the Director requested that a library representative be appointed to this committee, it did not happen although a librarian was chosen by the University Curriculum Committee as one of its representatives. CRUE's report and recommendations were disseminated for review and discussion and are, at present, being implemented. Only one of the seventy-two recommendations dealt specifically with the Libraries, but quite a few of the curriculum based recommendations will have significant implications when implemented (Council to Review Undergraduate Education 1988, 71). Significant curriculum review activities are resulting from CRUE and from a projected

FIGURE 1. The Vision of Michigan State University for the Year 2000. Source: Office of the Provost, Michigan State University

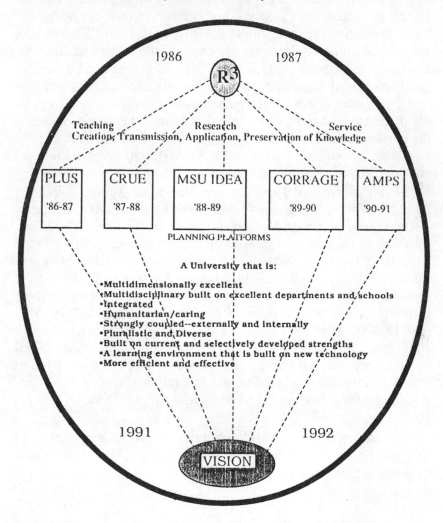

academic calendar change. Current and future Libraries planning documents will have to address the many issues posed by undergraduate curricular review and reform.

CORRAGE (Council on the Review of Research and Graduate Education) is presently underway and unfortunately, the Library once again is not represented on this committee. Each of the COR-RAGE subcommittees is expected to meet with the Director of Libraries to receive the Libraries' perspective on their recommendations. Following the same model as CRUE, this is an all-university, centralized initiative. Interestingly enough, the revised list of environmental tendencies provided to CORRAGE contained a number of controversial statements concerning libraries and information (e.g., "Private commercial ventures will establish themselves as the proprietors of large electronic data bases, eventually replacing the university library"[Michigan State University 1989b, 36-37]). It will be interesting to see how CORRAGE will involve Libraries staff in discussions of these issues.

IDEA (Institutional Diversity: Excellence in Action) initializes both centralized and decentralized planning processes. A centralized diversity plan was developed by staff in the Provost's Office. In addition, each major administrative unit was required to develop a "college level plan" relating to institutional diversity (Michigan State University 1989c; Michigan State University Office of the Provost 1989). Libraries' staff at all levels were involved in three planning committees: Climate, Program Planning, Displays (Shapiro 1989d). After the committee reports were disseminated to all staff, four open forums were held to discuss both the issues raised and the proposals for change. The Director then compiled a report that was forwarded to central administration (Davis 1990). Proposals requiring funding are to be included in the Libraries' annual budget request (APPR).

The final platform, AMPS (Administrative Management and Program Support), is scheduled to commence in 1990/91 and a process has not yet been formalized.

EXPECTED OUTCOMES OF R³

The President and Provost determined that the success of refocusing, rebalancing, and refining the University would be assessed according to the University's ability to:

- improve the quality of undergraduate education;
- restructure lifelong education programs into a truly lifelong learning process throughout the University;
- demonstrate increased growth rate of research activity;
- better support for supplies, services, facilities support for faculty;
- improve campus morale and internal sense of community;
- recognize pluralism and diversity as key dimensions of the University's value system in addition to being a set of personnel practices;
- openly use established governance and advisory structures for establishing and reaching consensus on the future of the University;
- improve the image of the University as a well managed institution;
- achieve fiscal integrity through budget savings;
- develop an agenda that complements that of state government;
- rekindle the service dimensions of the University's mission related to the creation, application, and dissemination of knowledge; and finally,
- expand ongoing communication and planning among and between academic and support units (Michigan State University 1989a, 9-10).

LIBRARY PLANNING WITHIN R³

The heart of the R³ process is the Academic Program & Planning Review (APPR) conducted by all academic units and Support Service Program Planning Review (SSPPR), conducted by all support service units. In February 1988, prior to developing APPR/SSPPR statements and while the R³ process was being formulated, all major administrative units (MAU) were asked to prepare three brief scenarios on how the MAU would look if within five years, 5%, 10%, or 15% of its base budget were to be reduced.

The particular roles and strengths of your unit should serve as the predicate for the changes which you consider, while keeping a clear eye toward the gestalt of MSU. . . . The consideration of these preliminary options should also be guided by the need to identify and communicate constraints internal to the academic enterprise, related to the support services, or external to the University which impinge upon and affect your planning. (Scott 1988a)

The following planning guidelines were outlined: the University's tripartite mission of teaching, research, and public service must be bridged with one another; Excellent faculty and programs must be full supported and nurtured; Utilize a multi-year planning context with budget reallocations of 4-8% likely in the first year up to 10-15% reallocations possible in out-years through 1990-91; Cooperative planning with other units is essential (Scott 1988a). Historically, the Libraries' materials budget has been excluded from budget reductions or call backs of funds and that was true in this instance as well.

After consulting with the Libraries' administrative group, the Director prepared a two page document indicating that budget reductions of the 10-15% magnitude would compromise seriously the University's ability to support a research library. The scenarios were described within the framework of the University's tripartite mission of research, teaching, and public services (see Figure 2).

The Provost responded to the Libraries' "think tank" document by providing budget guidelines and priorities to be considered when preparing the 1989 APPR: (1) all University reallocation targets would be in the 4.5-5.5% range, but through reallocation, the Libraries would receive 3-3.5% back for special line items such as providing inflationary increases for the materials budget; (2) a recognition of the "importance of the Libraries and the simultaneous need to look at the operating budget while protecting the book fund"; (3) it might be necessary to slow the development of automation in order to maintain basic services; and, (4) it will become increasingly necessary to "evaluate programs and identify those which are excellent and strong and must remain so, those which are weak but should be strengthened toward excellence, and those

FIGURE 2. From a February 24, 1988 letter from Richard E. Chapin, Director of Libraries to Provost David K. Scott and Associate Provost Lou Ann Simon.

GOAL

	INSTRUCTION	RESEARCH	SERVICE
Priorities would be:	- general reference service	- collections	- OPAC
	- bibliographic instruction	- new technology resources	- current collections
	- duplication in collections	- bibliographic access	- outreach services
	- hours	- OPAC	- spec. ref.
	- new tech. for services	- preservation	- fees for services
		- specialized reference	- document delivery

••

The logical redcutions would be:	- book fund	- bibliographic instruction	- preservation
	- preservation	- quick reference	- bibliog. instruction
	- OPAC	- non-print resources	hours
	- cataloging	- hours	- reference services

which are weak and should remain so or be eliminated'' (Scott 1988b).

The Libraries' subsequent APPR document became the basis for its FY89 budget allocation from the Provost and its internal goals and objectives plan for the year. In the final analysis, some additional dollars were reallocated to the Libraries both for automation to continue development of the OPAC though at a slower pace than originally planned and for the materials budget to cover inflation of serials. Five and a half positions in technical services and one collection development position were not filled based on program reductions identified in the APPR document and subsequently approved by the Provost.

By January 1989, the R³ document was fully developed and widely disseminated on campus and formally incorporated into the University's budget planning cycle. The Provost asked all Deans and separately reporting directors to submit an initial plan presenting options recommended for reconfiguring their units with both ten percent and fifteen percent budget reductions over the next three years prior to preparation of the unit's APPR (Scott 1989a). In addition, the plan was to identify new programmatic thrusts and revenue enhancement opportunities. Since the materials budget historically has been exempt from the Libraries base budget reductions, the cuts would result in approximately $610,000 and $915,000 reductions respectively to the Libraries' budget.

The units were allowed one month to develop their plans. For the Libraries, this time frame occurred while the Director was on a two month leave of absence. The Deputy Director, who led this process, operating within the participation principles outlined in R³, worked with the Libraries' senior administrators to develop a process that would involve as many library staff as possible.

What became evident immediately, was that the staff had no real knowledge or understanding of the various components of the Libraries' budget. Each unit knew what its own student or materials budgets consisted of, but the staff had no idea how much was spent by the Libraries on personnel, photocopying, equipment, or automation. In order to receive thoughtful and useful input from the staff, it was necessary to provide them with specific and detailed data on the various components of the Libraries' budget, something that heretofore had never been done.

A process for soliciting staff input was developed by the administrators and was presented to the Library Advisory Council (LAC), an elected body of librarians who advise the Director on issues of library policy. After consultation with the LAC, a memorandum was prepared and distributed to the entire staff summarizing the task as requested by the Provost, describing the process to be followed by the Libraries, summarizing the impact of the five percent base budget reduction received for the current fiscal year, and presenting a one page summary of the current Libraries budget (Shapiro 1989a).

The memorandum invited all staff to submit written comments on program priorities, areas for program or revenue enhancement, and areas for program reduction to either the Deputy Director, the Department Head, the Unit Head, or to a Library Advisory Council representative within ten days. Written communications did not have to be signed. In addition, group discussions were held in each department, led by the Department Head, over a two week period (concurrent with the timeframe for written communications).

The results of the written communications and group discussions were provided to the Library Advisory Council which then recommended priorities for inclusion in the Libraries' plan. Consensus was reached on the following priorities:

1. Maintain essential services:
   - keep building open (but with reduced hours)
   - keep materials shelved (physical accessibility)
   - keep materials acquired and catalogued (bibliographic accessibility)
   - maintain core reference services (I/R)
2. Maintain collections that support the University's programmatic needs (both materials budget and staff to implement it).
3. Complete implementation of [OPAC] (Michigan State University Libraries 1989b).

The LAC also discussed various revenue generating proposals, such as raising photocopy fees, and possible programmatic cuts, but little consensus could be reached on most of the proposals that were generated. Consensus was reached on areas of strength and new programmatic thrusts that needed to be reflected in the plan to the Provost (Michigan State University Libraries 1989c).

A preliminary document was prepared for and reviewed by the University Committee for the Library, an all-University elected advisory committee of faculty and students. This group supported the priorities identified by the LAC. All agreed that none of the proposed cuts were advisable and that library quality would be jeopardized. Nevertheless, consensus was reached on several proposals such as raising photocopy rates, reducing hours, and reducing specialized reference services (University Committee for the Library 1989).

The Deputy Director, with the assistance of the administrative group, prepared the reconfiguration plan for the Provost's Office (Shapiro 1989b). While the budget cutting proposals were discussed most by staff, other elements of the plan, such as highest program priorities for 89/90 -92/93, significant environmental constraints, short-run opportunities for savings or funding, also were discussed. For most staff, this was the first time they had been involved in such discussions.

A number of significantly undesirable program reductions had to be proposed under the fifteen percent reduction plan, including the closing of two branch libraries. Word spread like wild fire across campus that consideration was being given to closing branch libraries and both the Libraries and Provost Office were inundated with complaints. Even though neither branch had to be closed, the process produced a much needed dialogue between the Libraries and several key units on camps.

Once the reconfiguration plan was completed and forwarded to the Provost, the Deputy Director distributed a detailed summary to the staff and then met with each of the departments to discuss any residual issues of concern (Shapiro 1989c). These forums provided the Deputy Director with an opportunity to explain why many of the proposals for reduction were not included, why others were included, and what the priorities for the future would be. It also served to allay many of the fears of the staff concerning the process.

The report to the Provost initiated the dialogue on library funding that would continue over several months. It also initiated dialogue within the Libraries concerning not only budgets but also of the future programmatic directions of the Libraries. The process also provided the Director and Deputy Director with opportunities to discuss issues of common concern with other units on campus.

In subsequent meetings with the Provost concerning both the planning document and the Libraries' APPR, the discussion agenda was based on the issues identified in the reconfiguration document. The three year budget reallocation target for the Libraries was set at

two percent rather than the ten or fifteen percent originally proposed, however, several unexpected automation costs meant that
for the first year of the cycle the Libraries had to manage not only
the 2% reallocation to the Provost's Office but also a three percent
internal reallocation for automation. Due to the discussions held
concerning the reconfiguration communication, Libraries staff were
able to respond to the tight budget allocations for fiscal year 1990
with a better understanding of real world considerations. This was
particularly important at a time when a new director was assuming
leadership of the Libraries.

IMPLICATIONS OF THE R^3 PROCESS
FOR THE LIBRARIES

While it is too soon to tell how effective R^3 will be in truly reconfiguring Michigan State University to better address its mission as
we approach the twenty-first century, significant changes are being
implemented now in both undergraduate curriculum and lifelong
education. Undoubtedly, these changes will effect the Libraries and
it is unfortunate that the Libraries were not involved in developing
the process, but more importantly were also excluded from participation in the planning efforts themselves. The Libraries' role will
continue to be reactive to what is decided by others. Given the
current composition of the CORRAGE planning group, it is likely
that the same situation will result with the review of research and
graduate studies.

In late 1989, the first new Director of Libraries in thirty years
was appointed at Michigan State and planning is underway to implement a separate library strategic planning process during 1990.
This process will be incorporated into the R^3 process and will result
in the Libraries using the output resulting from all of the R^3 central
University planning efforts (Michigan State University Libraries
1990). In addition, the experiences gained by staff from all previous
planning efforts should facilitate the strategic planning process for
the new director.

While the Libraries staff have been involved with planning and
program evaluation activities within the Libraries for many years,

the lack of staff participation in budgetary planning has been a significant problem. The inclusion of all staff in budget planning during fiscal year 89 has had several residual benefits. First, the staff were better informed about the current state of library funding; and their program proposals and budget requests were more realistic than ever before. This contributed to reducing possible morale problems during an extremely tight budget year.

Second, the R³ exercise positioned the staff to move effectively into the strategic planning process being implemented by the new director. Because the approach was wholistic, viewing new priorities and program areas rather than merely budget cutting, the staff were encouraged to look towards the future despite a lean present. Frequently during times of tight budgets, staff are disinclined to address new program areas. The R³ strategic planning focus forces units to address the future even when there is not enough money to address all present needs. This "world view" is essential to the success of developing a strategic plan.

Third, the process has provided the Libraries with an effective platform from which the emphasize with University administrators the important role played by the Libraries in all academic enterprises. Because inter-unit cooperation is encouraged by the R³ process, a number of jointly sponsored projects have been proposed. Some of these were initiated by Libraries staff and others by other units on campus. In all instances, this resulted in other units including within their plans, library proposals.

And finally, the approach taken within the Library to educate the entire staff about the budgeting process, and then to involve the staff in discussions of significant issues about the future of the Libraries, provided them with a sense of empowerment.

According to the authors of *The Academic Intrapreneur*, "the most important challenge facing colleges and universities in the years ahead is the need to adopt and develop new programs, products, and technologies which we cannot even conceptualize today (Perlman 1988, 177-8). To accomplish this, the organizational culture must reflect the importance of trust, integrity, empowerment, and people (Perlman 1988, 172). As the staff approached the new decade and life with a new library director, the R³ process was used to begin to change the organizational culture of the Libraries to one more adaptable to changing environments and more capable of addressing future challenges.

NOTE

1. For a description of both long-range and strategic planning as they have evolved within higher education, see Cope, 1981 and Hesse, 1985.

REFERENCES

Chapin, Richard E. 1988. Memorandum to David K. Scott and Lou Anna K. Simon, February 24, 1988.

Committee on the Future of the University. 1959. Report to the President. East Lansing: Michigan State University.

Cope, Robert. 1981. Strategic Planning, Management, and Decision Making. AAHE-ERIC/Higher Education Research Report no. 9.

Council to Review Undergraduate Education. 1988. Opportunities for Renewal; Report of the Council to Review Undergraduate Education. East Lansing: Michigan State University.

Davis, Hiram L. 1990. MSU IDEA: Library Planning Program. East Lansing.

Hesse, Martha. 1985. The Development of a Long-Range and Strategic Planning Guide for a Large, Public University. Ph.D. diss., Michigan State University.

Long Range Planning Council. 1978. Report to the President on Long Range Planning. East Lansing: Michigan State University.

Michigan State University. 1984. Statement on Long Range Strategic Planning. East Lansing.

_____. 1989a. The Refocusing, Rebalancing, and Refining of Michigan State University; Internal Discussion Paper. East Lansing, January. Photocopy.

_____. 1989b. The Refocusing, Rebalancing, and Refining of Michigan State University; Internal Discussion Paper. East Lansing, October. Photocopy.

_____. 1989c. MSU IDEA. East Lansing: Draft 4/11/89 (Special Reissue 9/15/89).Photocopy.

Michigan State University Libraries. 1979. A Proposed Plan for Performance Evaluation in the Michigan State University Library. East Lansing. Photocopy.

_____. 1983. Report of the Public Services Study Team. East Lansing. Photocopy.

_____. 1989a. Library Advisory Council Minutes, 18 January 1989.

_____. 1989b. Library Advisory Council Minutes, 1 February 1989.

_____. 1989c. Library Advisory Council Minutes, 8 February 1989.

_____. 1989d. Library Advisory Council Minutes, 15 February 1989.

_____. 1990. Executive Summary of the Strategic Planning Retreat, January 11-12. Photocopy.

Michigan State University Office of the Provost. 1989. College Level Planning Program of the MSU IDEA. East Lansing.

Perlman, Baron, James Gueths, & Donald A. Weber. 1988. The Academic Intrapreneur; Strategy, Innovation, and Management in Higher Education. N.Y.: Praeger.

Scott, David K. 1988a. Letter to Richard E. Chapin, February 12, 1988.

_____. 1988b. Letter to Richard E. Chapin, May 11, 1988.

Shapiro, Beth J. 1989a. Memorandum to Library Staff on the Budget Planning Process, 17 January 1989.

_____. 1989b. Reconfiguring the Libraries/Archives at Reduction Levels of 10% and 15%; a communication to the Provost, 15 February 1989.

_____. 1989c. Reconfiguring the Libraries/Archives at Reduction Levels of 10% and 15%; a summary prepared for Libraries/Archives staff, 15 February 1989.

_____. 1989d. Memorandum on MSU-IDEA College Level Planning Program to Library Staff, 6 September 1989.

University Committee for the Library. 1989. Minutes of the 1 February 1989 meeting. East Lansing.

The University of Iowa Libraries' Strategic Plan

Barbara I. Dewey

SUMMARY. This article describes how the University of Iowa Libraries used strategic planning techniques to move forward in the development of crucial services in an environment of complex and expanding information resources. The result of the planning effort was a five year strategic plan integrating major University-wide goals of enhanced undergraduate education, diversity, premier graduate programs and excellent faculty.

INTRODUCTION

Librarians are recognizing that research libraries today need to be more than an access point to a physically static repository of information. Library staff need to have the tools to play a leadership role in handling increasingly complex knowledge bases by applying new technologies and methods of inquiry. Librarians should implement programs that provide the kind of comprehensive information literacy urgently needed by students and faculty. Library organizational design should provide maximum opportunity to connect users to a wide range of information sources and retrieval methods. Librarians need to be prepared to play a major role in how new knowledge is created.

The University of Iowa Libraries is using strategic planning techniques to determine methods to move forward in these critical areas. The strategic plan of the Libraries articulates its aspirations and directions for the University over the next five years (see Appendix A). This paper describes experiences of the library staff in the initial cycle of strategic planning culminating in a five year strategic plan

Barbara I. Dewey is Director, Administrative and Access Services, University of Iowa Libraries.

99

coordinated through a university-wide planning process described elsewhere in this issue. The plan outlines the central place the library system has in the academic programs of the University, and suggests ways to more effectively integrate consideration of collections and services into these programs.

BACKGROUND

The University of Iowa Libraries system consists of the Main Library and 11 departmental libraries. The Main Library provides the services and collections for the social sciences and the humanities. Other units in the system include the Hardin Library for the Health Sciences, Art, Music, Business, Engineering, Geology, Biology, Chemistry/Botany, Psychology, Math, and Physics. A number of external groups advise the Libraries. The advisory committee to the University Libraries is appointed by President Rawlings and consists of faculty, student and staff members.

DESIGNING A LIBRARY FUTURE: THE PLANNING EFFORT BEGINS

New leadership, in early 1987, provided the impetus for a concerted library strategic planning effort. Certainly, planning was urgently needed. During the early 1980s the library experienced a drastic reduction in staffing resulting in the loss of 17 positions, or slightly more than ten percent of the full-time staff. Even before these cuts were initiated the University Libraries ranked 40th in professional and 66th in nonprofessional staffing but 29th in collections size according to the 1980/81 Association for Research Libraries statistics.[1] By 1987 the Libraries had not gained much ground and, added to this serious staffing storage was the implementation of OASIS, (Online Access for Information Sources), the library automation system and efforts to develop new initiatives while maintaining traditional services. Additionally library administrators and staff were eager to implement more comprehensive user education programs and acquire information resources in electronic format so as to provide the most efficient methods of retrieval for the campus. These pressing concerns had to be addressed in a logical, forthright and productive way using the talents of the staff to full advantage.

Sheila D. Creth, University Librarian, initiated the planning process in 1987 by inviting Duane Webster, then Director, Office of Management Studies (OMS), Association of Research Libraries (ARL), to lead a leadership development and planning seminar for library administrators and senior staff. The seminar, in the form of a retreat, provided participants with a process to critically examine the library's history, its current situation, and alternative futures described in the document, "Designing a Library Future: The University of Iowa Libraries, 1989-1997." The document identified four key result areas (KRAs) where success is essential for long term viability, where improvements must be made and where effort will bring the greatest benefit.[2] Four key result areas were identified: technology, outreach, staff development/personnel, and resource sharing/collection management. Each KRA constituted a group effort. After the seminar, group participants met individually and refined the definitions of the key result areas. The KRAs, combined with the library future statement, constituted the original framework for the first planning cycle and were the basis of departmental goals and objectives.

Other studies during this time contributed to the final library strategic plan. A plan was completed in late 1987 by an outside consultant on space in the Main Library, and later revised with a task force of library staff. A staffing utilization study, completed in March 1988, constituted the basis for additional staffing requests found in the plan. In early September 1988, a report, "Strengthening Library Services for the Undergraduate Student at The University of Iowa: a Compendium of Modest Measures," was prepared for the Vice President for Academic Affairs as an indication of the role the Libraries ought to play in the education of undergraduate students. (This report was requested by the Acting Vice President for Academic Affairs in relation to the University's focus on undergraduate education and its plan to direct a major funding request to the Iowa Board of Regents in support of a renewed effort to address the needs of undergraduates.) Although this proposal did not result in any additional staffing resources, it did serve to identify several priorities within the strategic plan.

DEVELOPING GOALS AND OBJECTIVES

During 1987/88 the Planning Group reviewed, revised and approved the KRA documents and prioritized activities within each KRA. The primary focus within each broad group was identified as follows:

PERSONNEL

comprehensive staff development programs
improved systems for evaluation and compensation
refined systems for consultation and information exchange

TECHNOLOGY

integrated library system
personal computer support
electronic information retrieval

OUTREACH

comprehensive user education programs
fund raising
public relations programs for the campus and external community

RESOURCE SHARING/COLLECTION MANAGEMENT

collection development policy
collection development administrative structure
resources sharing
preservation

Concurrently units throughout the system developed department goals and objectives for the next 18 month period. Department heads provided the link between the key result areas and operational goals. Eighteen months was chosen to allow sufficient time for evaluation and achievement of the first cycle of goal setting. Following this process, professional staff set individual goals that were to reflect, whenever possible, unit and system-wide goals.

Goals and objectives from all units were collected by the planning process coordinator and compiled into a master list for an overall review by the Planning Group during the summer of 1988. This gave library administrators and the Planning Group an opportunity to judge the overall appropriateness and impact of the goals/objectives and to make necessary adjustments. The Planning Group also advised the University Librarian in identifying options for reductions in service in order to cope with budget constraints. In 1988/89 there was no relief for a long-term inadequate general expense budget resulting in reductions in student hours to offset increased costs in supplies and services, and a University-wide position freeze further affected staffing. Finally, a 8.3% increase was allocated for the materials budget, requiring yet another round of serials cuts and reduction of monographic purchases due to extradordinary price increases (the Planning Group was not specifically involved in the materials budget allocations).

SHIFTING GEARS: INTEGRATION
OF THE UNIVERSITY-WIDE PLANNING EFFORT

The University-wide strategic planning initiative was announced during the fall of 1988. The University Libraries was one of 22 first level campus planning units asked to submit individual strategic plans to the newly formed University Strategic Planning Committee. Edward Lawler, Chair of the committee, was asked to speak at the February 1989 retreat to the Planning Group about the university-wide process. This gave the Planning Group an opportunity to ask Mr. Lawler specific questions about how the University Libraries would fit into the overall university plan. Participants were particularly concerned that issues related to library resources and services be integrated into other first level planning documents. Mr. Lawler also announced areas of primary institutional focus for the University. The final document listed the arts, basic science and technological innovation, human and environmental health, literature, discourse and critical analysis and social change as priorities.

The retreat also served as a mid-year review and accomplished the following: examined progress of priority programs identified by the Planning Group in the documents, "Designing a Library Future" and "Key Result Area Annotated Summary;" determined further work needed and the priority for topics in each key result area; linked progress of general priority programs to progress being made in departments and addressed other key departmental issues;

determined future review mechanisms for the planning process; and revised planning documents.

After the February 1989 planning retreat the KRA groups revised their documents and selected representatives from each group who met with the coordinator of the planning process to determine how the KRAs could be integrated into the strategic planning document to be submitted to the University (an initial draft by May 1, 1989). A draft document was produced which attempted to integrate the KRAs into a goals and objectives framework for the entire library system. Additionally the group needed to consider how to integrate institutional goals defined by the campus-wide committee. These included: comprehensive strength in undergraduate programs, premier graduate and professional programs in a number of areas, faculty of national and international distinction, an academic community diverse in gender, race, ethnicity, and nationality, strong ties with external constituencies, and a high quality of life.

This first attempt, while valuable for framing previous work into a single document, had a number of weaknesses. First, the KRAs were not intended to cover all operational concerns and indeed, certain library operations were not even addressed directly within the KRA framework. Secondly, the KRAs were not written for a wider audience and thus did not always take into consideration the primary service orientation of the library. Therefore, a major rewriting of the strategic plan took place. The centrality of a library information network to the quality of education at the University was the underlying concept in developing the rewritten plan. Additionally, the eventual readers of the plan, university administrators, library users, and state officials were considered as every section of the plan was further developed. The plan, after being reviewed by the Planning Group, at library staff mettings and by the faculty/staff advisory committee, was submitted on May 1, 1989 to the University Strategic Planning Committee.

ASSUMPTIONS AND MAJOR THEMES
IN THE PLAN

The executive summary preceding the plan outlined important assumptions underlying the plan:

The strategic plan of the University Libraries has been developed with the view that an outstanding library is central to the quality and accomplishments of the University as a whole. The plan assumes, therefore, that the library will be a top priority of the University because of the integral role it plays in the educational and research mission of the University. Further, if it is a major goal for the University to become a premier institution of higher education, then attention must be given to creating a library system that will support the achievement of this goal.

The library plan describes nine goals and accompanying strategies which if implemented would provide a range of services and information resources that would support and enhance instruction and research for the campus community, and permit the Libraries to contribute more effectively to the State at large. The goals are interrelated and should be viewed as equally important.

In an increasingly complex information society with an expanding base of published and unpublished materials in a variety of formats, creating a strong and dynamic library and information network is critical. This will not be possible without addressing the more than a decade of seriously inadequate funding for support of library staff and collections which in turn has resulted in less than adequate library services essential to a large research university.[3]

The goals in the plan reflected both university-wide areas of focus and issues and concepts related to research library staff across the country. Themes within the Libraries' plan included: enhanced information literacy for undergraduate students through educational programs, recognition and the means to develop a diverse staff within an increasingly diverse campus community, integration of changing formats and technologies into the collections (fully supported in all respects), and appropriate staff development and training to more adequately support research from all types of users; the need for all planning and major college and department initiatives to incorporate library resource implications; and development of an increased awareness of library services and needs in the external community.

Resources required in dollars and positions for specific objectives within each goal were identified and these totaled $3,985,876 in recurring and $6,844,947 in nonrecurring funding. Additionally $19,864,000 in nonrecurring funds was included for the construction of a combined science library building.

While these resources might seem large, they did not represent a wish list including a vast array of state-of-the art technology but described an honest assessment of what would actually be required in staff and other resources to make enough progress to begin to support an excellent research university.

THE FINAL DRAFT – RESOURCE SCENARIOS

The committee returned the plan asking for minimal clarification and requesting (for all university first level planning units) that three scenarios be added concerning what the library could accomplish with a: (1) 15% increase to its budget: (2) 5% increase added; or (3) 5% decrease. Requests for additional funding required to carry out specific objectives were also to be placed in priority order in a five year sequence.

ACHIEVING DISTINCTION

As the library was completing the final draft of its plan the university-wide committee had submitted the draft of the University's plan, *Achieving Distinction*, for review by campus units and individuals. The University Libraries' plan was reflected as a high priority throughout this document. The university committee recognized the importance of integrating library concerns with academic planning at all levels. The library planning committee did have a few concerns about the final document. The word "library" was often separated from the phrase "information technology." Information resources irrespective of format or technology base are the concern of libraries. Access and management of these information resources remains a central goal of the University of Iowa Libraries working in concert with other campus units that assist in the provision of the necessary technology to access these resources.

STRATEGIC PLANNING INITIATIVE PROPOSALS

The President and the Acting Vice President for Academic Affairs did not want the university planning document to remain a collection of paper dreams. During the fall of 1989 they called for innovative and collaborative proposals from departments and individuals across the campus to be considered for funding from a pool of $1,000,000 (strategic planning initative fund). The University Libraries submitted six proposals to the university administration. Four proposals were developed by the library administration with the assistance of faculty and staff (from a wide range of disciplines) and two other proposals were developed by the Engineering Librarian: The first of four projects was for a Hypermedia Information Design Project. This project seeks to establish a focus within the University Libraries to integrate the latest computer software applications, specifically hypermedia, to create dynamic products that will enhance the understanding and use of library services and information resources; second, a proposal to create a Learning Center for Interactive Technology in the Main Library, a facility to expand and integrate a number of learning and research activities using the latest in information technology to prepare students for the future; third, funding to hire a Minority/Special Services Librarian to establish a coordinated effort within the University Libraries to address the needs of minority students and students at risk academically or who have special needs related to the effective use and integration of library and information resources into their educational program; and fourth, providing access to journal indexes through the library online system. Proposals from the Engineering Librarian were for equipment to load public domain materials online in the Engineering Library; and to establish a *virtual* environmental sciences library to meet the increasing information needs of students and faculty in this discipline.

FUTURE USES OF THE UNIVERSITY LIBRARIES' STRATEGIC PLAN

The University Libraries' strategic plan is currently used in a number of ways: (1) it provides the overall conceptual framework for the current and future allocation of library resources and services; (2) it serves as the basis for ongoing library strategic planning; (3) it serves as the basis for budget proposals to the university administration and the state legislature; (4) it provides ideas and directions for the identification of projects suitable for external funding opportunities; and (5) it serves as an informational piece about the University Libraries.

The strategic planning process is more than an exercise for the staff of the University of Iowa Libraries and the campus. It is providing the catalyst for the achievement of excellence at the University of Iowa. The recognized centrality and critical importance of a strong library is a clear outcome of the Iowa planning effort. Achievement of the goals and objectives stated in the plan over the next five years will truly be the mark of a successful library and campus planning effort.

NOTES

1. Association for Research Libraries. *ARL Statistics 1980/81* (Washington, D.C.: ARL, 1981).

2. University of Iowa Libraries. *Designing a Library Future: The University of Iowa Libraries, 1987-1997.* (Iowa City, University of Iowa Libraries: 1987).

3. "Executive Summary," *University of Iowa Libraries Strategic Plan.* (Iowa City, University of Iowa Libraries: 1989).

APPENDIX A

THE UNIVERSITY OF IOWA LIBRARIES STRATEGIC PLAN - SUMMARY OF MISSION AND
GOALS

Mission

THE UNIVERSITY LIBRARIES IS THE CENTRAL UNIVERSITY INSTITUTION
SUPPORTING THE DEVELOPMENT AND DELIVERY OF LIBRARY AND
INFORMATION RESOURCES, AND THE PRESERVATION OF KNOWLEDGE. THE
MISSION OF THE UNIVERSITY LIBRARIES IS TO PROVIDE COLLECTION
AND STAFF RESOURCES IN SUPPORT OF TEACHING, RESEARCH, SERVICE
AND PUBLIC OUTREACH, AND TO RESPOND TO THE NEED OF ALL MEMBERS
OF THE UNIVERSITY COMMUNITY TO BE LIBRARY AND INFORMATION
LITERATE.

APPENDIX A (continued)

Goals

Goal #1 - UNDERGRADUATE STUDENTS DEVELOP LIBRARY AND INFORMATION SKILLS
USING TRADITIONAL MATERIALS AND STATE OF THE ART INFORMATION TECHNOLOGY TO
ACHIEVE SUCCESS IN ACADEMIC PURSUITS AND TO PREPARE FOR A CHANGING WORLD.

Goal #2 - FACULTY, STUDENT AND STAFF RESEARCH ARE FULLY SUPPORTED THROUGH
COMPREHENSIVE DISCIPLINE-BASED SERVICES.

Goal #3 - PROFESSIONAL STAFF OF DISTINCTION AND A WELL-TRAINED SUPPORT
STAFF REPRESENTING DIVERSITY IN ALL REGARDS ARE RECRUITED AND RETAINED IN
APPROPRIATE NUMBERS.

Goal #4 - COLLECTIONS FULLY SUPPORT CURRENT AND CHANGING TEACHING AND RESEARCH NEEDS OF THE UNIVERSITY, AND ARE ACCESSIBLE IN A VARIETY OF FORMATS AND TECHNOLOGIES.

Goal #5 - INFORMATION TECHNOLOGY IS INTEGRATED INTO ALL ASPECTS OF THE COLLECTIONS, THE PROVISION OF SERVICES AND ACCESS TO LIBRARY AND INFORMATION RESOURCES ON CAMPUS AND ELSEWHERE.

Goal #6 - PHYSICAL FACILITIES PROVIDE EFFICIENT SPACE FOR THE HOUSING AND PRESERVATION OF COLLECTIONS AND THE PROVISION OF SERVICES.

Goal #7 - LIBRARY COLLECTIONS AND SERVICES ARE AN INTEGRAL PART OF ALL

PLANNING AND MAJOR INITIATIVES BY ACADEMIC COLLEGES, DEPARTMENTS AND

PROGRAMS.

Goal #8 - DEVELOPMENT AND PUBLIC RELATIONS PROGRAMS INCREASE THE VISIBILITY

OF UNIVERSITY LIBRARIES SERVICES AND COLLECTIONS TO NUMEROUS

CONSTITUENCIES.

Goal #9 - THE UNIVERSITY LIBRARIES, AS THE STATE'S LARGEST LIBRARY,

SUPPORTS THE UNIVERSITY'S INITIATIVES IN INFORMATION TRANSFER AND THE

STATE'S EFFORTS IN ECONOMIC DEVELOPMENT.

112

The Library Long-Range Planning Process at Wayne State

Eileen M. Mulhare

SUMMARY. The article presents a chronicle of the long-range planning process undertaken by the Wayne State University Library System from January 1988 through April 1989. The sixteen-month planning period included two retreats as well as a lengthy document preparation stage. Participants were rewarded with a public document that reflects the Library System's aspirations and has carried its message to constituencies around the country. The author suggests how the planning timetable might have been shortened in five areas: developing the background materials; formation of assumptions; defining key results sought; structuring the final document; and organization of the writing process.

THE INSTITUTIONAL SETTING

Wayne State University is a Carnegie Commission-ranked research institution and a constitutionally autonomous component of the Michigan state system of higher education. As an urban university, Wayne State serves the needs of an ethnically and racially diverse student population, drawn primarily from the city of Detroit and its metropolitan environs. Enrollment in fall 1989 totaled 32,477, including 20,592 undergraduates and 11,885 students in graduate and professional programs.

The Wayne State University Library System is comprised of four libraries, each housed in separate facilities: Purdy/Kresge Library, which serves as the main library; Science and Engineering Library;

Eileen M. Mulhare is the former Director of Grants and Development, Wayne State University Library System, Wayne State University, Detroit, MI. Correspondence may be addressed to the author at P.O. Box 215, Hamilton, NY.

which serves as the main library; Science and Engineering Library; Arthur Neef Law Library; and Vera Shiffman Medical Library. The Library System also operates the Pharmacy and Allied Health Learning Resources Center, managed by Shiffman Medical Library, and the Federal Mogul Library Annex storage facility. Total collections include over 2.2 million bound volumes, 1.8+ million microforms, and more than 23,000 current subscriptions to journals and government publications.

THE DECISION TO PLAN STRATEGICALLY

The Library System undertook a comprehensive self-study from July 1982 through June 1983. A major goal of this effort was to establish uniform operating policies and procedures for all four libraries in preparation for automation. The self-study report, published in August 1983, resembled a long-range plan in some respects. It presented a seven-point mission statement, eighteen assumptions and eight goals. Instead of identifying system-wide objectives, however, the self-study was accompanied by fifty-six pages of charts listing tasks to be carried out at the unit level within the next two to three years.

The Library System began its first formal long-range planning process in 1983. Three factors contributed to the timing of this decision. The first was the recent appointment of a new Director of Libraries, later to become the Dean of Libraries and Library Science. Second, Wayne State University policy requires that a Provost-appointed Review Committee evaluate the progress of the Library System every five years. The evaluation for 1979-1983 was scheduled to occur in 1983. Finally, the President of Wayne State, in his budget notes for FY 1984, specifically asked the Director of Libraries to prepare a long-range plan for presentation to the university Board of Governors.

Three groups participated in reviewing preliminary versions of the 1984-1988 Long-Range Plan: the professional staff of the libraries; the Administrative Council, later known as the Libraries Management Group, composed of Library System top management; and the University Library Committee, a faculty advisory body. The final document was completed in August 1984.

In contrast to the earlier self-study, the 1984-1988 Long-Range Plan looked beyond unit-level considerations and focused on system-wide issues. The mission statement which had earlier referred only to "users" now identified the users the Library System seeks to serve: faculty and students; business and industry; the community in general and other libraries. The assumptions underlying the plan were separated into two categories: those related to information management principles; and those distinctive to library operations at Wayne State. Only three goals were forwarded: automating operations and services; strengthening collections, services and facilities; and establishing an ongoing program to attract external funding through gifts and grants. Listed under each goal was a set of objectives and related implementation strategies.

With the 1984-1988 Long-Range Plan, the Library System began an integrated five-year cycle of planning, implementation and evaluation which continues to the present.

DESIGNING THE PLANNING PROCESS

Preparations for the next long-range plan, to cover the period from 1989 through 1993, were initiated by the Dean of Libraries and Library Science in January 1988. Like the first long-range plan, this second effort would produce a document to: assist the university administration in its budgetary and overall institutional planning; propose specific, measurable goals for the Library System to achieve over the next five years; and furnish the next Provost's Review Committee with benchmarks against which to rate the advancement of the Library System.

Unlike the 1984-1988 document, however, the 1989-1993 Long-Range Plan had a fourth purpose, to inform external audiences of the Library System's mission, goals and objectives. As will be seen later in this discussion, choosing to make the plan a public document lengthened the timetable needed to complete the planning process.

In a memorandum to the librarians on January 20, 1988, the Dean asked them to begin thinking about the libraries' mission, future goals and objectives, and to start discussing ideas and proposals at the unit level. A copy of the 1984-1988 Long-Range Plan was enclosed. At the same time, he announced that a more structured planning process would be undertaken later in the year with the assistance of an outside consultant. Engaging the services of a facilitator and advisor would "allow broad and knowledgeable participation by a large segment of [the Library System's] staff and librarians." The consultant chosen was the new Executive Director of the Association of Research Libraries and former head of ARL/ OMS, the Association's Office of Management Studies.

As originally conceived, the planning process was to take about six months. In January, the Dean would announce the planning initiative to the staff and select an outside consultant. In February, the consultant would make a preliminary visit to interview key Library System personnel. In March, the consultant would provide the Dean with a detailed proposal for the planning process. This would be followed by appointment of an in-house planning team, comprised of librarians, administrators and other staff members. A retreat for the planning team would be held in May, led by the consultant and aimed at drafting the plan. The planning team would meet with the consultant for a second retreat in June to make revisions and adopt the final document.

As scheduled, the consultant arrived on February 23 for two days of meetings. Private interviews were conducted with the ten members of the Libraries Management Group. This body consists of the Dean, the heads of the four libraries, the Director of the Automation Systems Office, the Director of Technical Services, the Director of Grants and Development, the Director of Business Operations and the Personnel Officer. The two librarians in charge of the Center for Bibliographic Instruction were also interviewed. The pre-planning visit included two group sessions as well. The consultant held a joint meeting of public service and technical services librarians to discuss collection development and organization issues. At a meeting for all Library System managers, librarians and staff, the consultant gave a presentation on the programs and services available through ARL/OMS.

The outcome of the pre-planning visit was a two-page proposal, prepared by the consultant on March 9. It detailed the purpose, tentative agenda, arrangements and format for a Leadership Development Program, the new name for the scheduled May and June retreats.

The proposal suggested seven general areas for discussion by participants in the Leadership Development Program: pressures for change and alternative responses; values and service philosophy; improving service delivery within existing resource restraints; clarification of organizational responsibilities; atmosphere for users and staff; balancing staff participation with effective leadership; and enhancing creativity and innovation.

The consultant's proposed agenda for the retreats consisted of eight topics: Library System history, traditions and current practices; trends in higher education, research and instruction; forces for change in research libraries; problems, issues and concerns facing the Library System; strategic planning concepts and methods; organizational and individual values; the process of organizational change; and formal and informal communication channels and processes within the library.

The Leadership Development Program proposal was accompanied by a ten-page ARL/OMS handout. It described four "alternative futures" for research libraries, distinguished from one another on the basis of university context, library philosophy and role, strategic concerns and staffing issues. The handout was intended for distribution before the first retreat convened in May, to allow participants two months to consider the implications of the four management models.

The members of the Libraries Management Group were advised in mid-March that planning retreats would be held in May and June. The other thirteen personnel appointed by the Dean to participate in the Leadership Development Program were notified two weeks before the May 16-17 retreat.

Initially, what would later be known as the Long-Range Planning Team consisted of twenty-three people. In addition to the Dean and the nine other members of the Libraries Management Group, these were: the assistant director of each of the four libraries; four more librarians from the main library; three technical services librarians; one automation systems librarian; and an assistant professor from the graduate Library Science Program. Two new team members were added in time for the second and final planning retreat, the newly-appointed Associate Dean of Libraries and a budget analyst from Library Business Operations.

THE FIRST PLANNING RETREAT

The initial Leadership Development Program retreat, held May 16-17, 1988, consisted of a series of exercises to encourage creative discussion and build confidence in the planning program.

The first day began with an overview of the planning process. The consultant defined planning as developing a view of a preferred future, including a vision, mission, goals, objectives, priorities and key result areas. He differentiated long-range planning from strategic planning. The former is an incremental rearrangement of elements while the latter is a transformation in which elements are not only rearranged but also added or deleted.[1] The benefits of planning were considered, such as more effective use of resources, as well as potential hazards, such as allowing planning to become an end in itself.

Early in the day, the planning team agreed that the original timetable for completing the 1989-1993 Long-Range Plan was unrealistic. The next retreat was scheduled for the last week in June, three weeks later than planned. The deadline for a solid draft of the plan was moved forward to August.

After reviewing the planning process the consultant, now taking the role of facilitator, suggested certain ground rules to be followed in the discussion group exercises which would form the balance of the first day. Among the rules were respecting each person's right to speak, actively listening to what is said, preserving confidentiality and mutual commitment, adhering to the time frame and maintaining an egalitarian attitude toward each other.

The twenty-three participants then were divided randomly into four discussion groups of five to six members. Each group selected its own facilitator to coordinate discussion, a recorder to take notes on a flip chart tablet, and a reporter to summarize the deliberations. These three roles were rotated with each new exercise.

The first assignment had the discussion groups list the achievements and shortfalls of the 1984-1988 Long-Range Plan. The second exercise asked the groups to identify threats and opportunities the Library System will face over the next three to five years. The next assignment was a "survival" game which served to demonstrate the effectiveness of group decision making over individual efforts.

The final exercise of the day involved the alternative futures handout which had accompanied the consultant's original proposal. For each of the four library management models detailed in the handout, the discussion groups were asked to: come up with a descriptive label; numerically rate the likelihood that the Library System would resemble the model someday; separately rate the desirability of the model; and identify the model's useful features.

The agenda for the second day began with a review of the previous day's proceedings, followed by two new exercises. The bellwether exercise encouraged discussion groups to define the ideal characteristics of a leading research library and to name libraries that seem to fit one or more of these criteria. The preferred futures exercise asked each discussion group to propose a model for the Library System by adapting one of the alternative futures models examined a day earlier. In the process, participants were required to: predict future conditions related to the university, the structure of the library, demographics, the economy and technology; agree on concepts underlying the model they selected, such as overall philosophy, response to technology, collection philosophy, and the role of the library in the university; identify strategic concerns; and suggest performance measures. Each of the four discussion groups prepared a five-minute oral presentation to explain its hybrid model to the rest of the planning team.

The May Leadership Development Program concluded with preparations for the next retreat. Members of the four discussion groups were reappointed to one of five new work groups. The membership of each work group consisted of at least one representative from each of the previous discussion groups.

The new work groups were given specific research and writing assignments to be completed before the June retreat. The Futures Group was responsible for a statement envisioning the Library System of the future. The Mission and Objectives Group would review the 1984-1988 Long-Range Plan together with the university's own mission statement (adopted in 1985) and recommend revisions to the Library System mission and objectives statements.[2] The Assumptions Group would examine the assumptions underlying the previous Long-Range Plan and propose any necessary modifications. The Environment Group would generate an overview of external factors affecting the university and its libraries over the next five to ten years. The Situation Group would assess the Library System's current capabilities, needs and expectations. Each work group was asked to prepare a draft report of no more than five pages for distribution at the June retreat.

THE SECOND PLANNING RETREAT

The next and final Leadership Development Program retreat was held June 23-24, 1988. The first day was devoted almost entirely to detailed consideration of the materials prepared by the five work groups. Four of the five work group reports (Futures, Mission and Objectives, Environment, and Situation) drew similar types of comments and criticisms. There was little argument about the substance of these presentations. It was agreed, however, that the next versions of these four documents must do a better job of separating factual statements from hypothetical scenarios and recommendations for future action. Changes in wording or emphasis were requested. Participants also identified logical inconsistencies, missing information and essential matters not yet addressed.

In contrast, the Assumptions Group statement elicited a lengthy exchange of ideas and substantial debate. The other work groups had focused largely on their own specific assignments. The Assumptions Group instead covered topics which overlapped the other four reports: the relation of the university and society to the Library System; the role of technology; library operations and management; collections and preservation; service programs; personnel; and resource sharing. Of course, all the work group reports had been based on some set of assumptions. But this was not recognized by the planning team until the Assumptions Group document was discussed. In the process, the retreat participants discovered the unstated and sometimes conflicting assumptions each work group employed in developing its particular report.

Towards the end of the day, the facilitator introduced the concept of "key result area" as a domain in which success is imperative, improvement is necessary and/or concerted effort will yield the greatest benefit. Examples offered of key result areas were collection development, public service, application of technology, fund development, faculty relations and staff development. The day closed with a homework assignment: each participant was asked to prepare a list of five key result areas.

The following day began with the five work groups meeting separately to plan the second draft of their reports. The focus then moved to the issue of key result areas for the Library System. Each work group was asked to develop a list of key result areas based on items proposed by its individual members. All five work groups subsequently compared their proposals to arrive at a definitive list.

The planning team as a whole agreed to incorporate five key result areas in the final list. Staffing strategy considered issues such as size, recruitment, retention, use, professional development, morale and training. Information services covered access, networks, delivery, technology and quality assurance. The collections area encompassed management and bibliographic concerns, preservation and space utilization. Fund development entailed internal and external funding sources as well as specific strategies. External relations was initially defined as involving user education, liaison functions and faculty relations. The category was later expanded to include public relations efforts such as news releases, special events and publications. This inventory of five key areas for improvement and enhancement ultimately formed the core of the 1989-1993 Long-Range Plan.[3]

For the next activity, the work groups were reshuffled. Members were reassigned to one of five new KRA (key result area) groups. Each KRA group was comprised of one representative from each of the five earlier work groups. Using a six-step process entitled STRIDE, each KRA group took responsibility for further developing its assigned key result area (staffing, information services, collections, fund development or external relations).

The STRIDE exercise suggested six major questions for the KRA groups to consider in relation to a key result area: what is the current situation; what is the target; what are the reasons or restraints preventing progress; what are the key ideas needed to arrive at a workable strategy; what exactly must be done, by whom and when; and how will success be evaluated.

The June retreat concluded with a timetable for completing the 1989-1993 Long-Range Plan. The Director of Grants and Development was appointed by the Dean to serve as long-range plan editor. In three weeks (mid-July), the work groups were expected to submit the second draft of the Futures, Mission and Objectives, Assumptions, Environment and Situation reports. These would be circulated to all planning team members, who were required to return comments to the long-range plan editor by the end of July. In turn, the editor was charged with the task of consolidating the five work group drafts into one report by mid-August.

On the matter of key result areas, the KRA groups formed at the June retreat would not meet again. Instead, the heads of the Library System's six major units (four libraries, Automation Systems and Technical Services) were asked to specify in writing by mid-August how the five KRAs would be implemented in their particular units. These new KRA documents would be distributed to all planning team members. As in the case of the work group reports, comments were due in two weeks (end of August) and should be addressed to the long-range plan editor. The editor was responsible for integrating the KRA documents with the combined work group materials into a final, focused document by mid-September. The date for completing the 1989-1993 Long-Range Plan, originally set for June and later advanced to August, now was slated for September.

GENERATING THE PLAN

By mid-August, the materials turned over to the editor consisted of five work group reports spanning a total of seventy pages and another twenty pages of KRA reports from the six library units. To facilitate editing, rewrites and typesetting, all text was submitted on diskette. For a variety of reasons which will be discussed momentarily, arriving at a definitive version of the 1989-1993 Long-Range Plan took six drafts produced over the next eight months. The plan in its final form consisted of a nineteen-page essay divided into twelve sections and accompanied by a two-page bibliography.

In the earliest stages of the writing process, numerous drafts were necessary because the May and June retreats had provided no suggestions on how to organize the document. Draft I, completed in mid-October, assumed that the plan must follow the same structure as the materials submitted. It presented slightly edited versions of the work groups' reports on Futures, Mission and Objectives, Assumptions, Environment and Situation, as well as an entirely new section on Key Results sought system-wide, gleaned from items in the unit-level KRA reports. Included also were the unit-level KRA reports, somewhat rewritten to follow a more consistent format.

When Draft I was circulated to members of the Libraries Management Group for comments the reactions were not encouraging. The principal criticisms were redundancies in the text. As the Associate Dean put it, "The segments were prepared as self-contained units; it is almost inevitable that key issues appear over and over again." There was also the problem of length. Of the sixty pages in Draft I, almost two-thirds would be cut by the time Draft II appeared.

None of the readers suggested that the current structure of the manuscript be revised. It was apparent, however, that the components in Draft I did not hang together in any rational way. The section on Key Results, both system-wide and for the various units, bore little relationship to the preceding sections on Assumptions, Environment, Situation and so forth. With the exception of the Mission and Objectives document, most of the work group reports were simply background materials to set the stage for the actual plan. The central argument of the plan, a detailed statement on what would be done, how and why, had not yet been written.

The editor undertook a fundamental restructuring of the work group materials for Draft II, which was completed in early December. Using the key results areas as a starting point and with the help of a computer, the Futures, Assumptions, Environment and Situation work group reports were disassembled. With additional research, the materials were rewritten and regrouped into six categories: Information, Technology and Networking; Collections and Preservation; Facilities; Information Services; Human Resources; and External Funding and External Relations.[4] For example, all assumptions associated with human resources were now to be found in that section of the text.

The Mission and Objectives statement, revised and expanded, was renamed Mission and Goals to more accurately reflect its content. The reorganization of the background materials for Draft II had reduced this portion of the text to less than twenty typewritten pages. It also answered the central questions of what the Library System hoped to achieve over the next five years and why.

The issue that remained unresolved in Draft II was how the plan's goals would be accomplished. This was the function of the Key Results section, the text of which had undergone only minor editorial changes from the first to the second draft. Most of the content was still fragmented into unit-level documents. The key results presented in Draft II were not specific enough to be considered guidelines for action. The system-wide discussion of key results was especially vague. It repeated goals already presented in the introductory sections of the plan but did not offer a comprehensive set of quantifiable targets.

With Draft III (early January 1989) and Draft IV (mid-January), the Dean of Libraries and Library Science and the Associate Dean set to work on rethinking the Key Results section. By Draft IV, the unit-level key results pages were dropped in favor of strengthening the description of key results sought system-wide. Special attention was given to explaining how the Library System would achieve and measure success in: collection development, management and access; facilities; information and access services; human resources; external relations; and funding strategies. Using an outline format, the Key Results section was distilled into six pages of action statements. The final form of the plan had begun to emerge.

Like Draft I, Draft IV of the plan was distributed to the Libraries Management Group for comments. This time, the Dean provided a set of questions for the reviewers to consider. How well does the plan reflect our ambitions? Does it cover all significant programs, present and future? Is it "overly ambitious, just right or too comfortable?" Should anything be added or deleted? The consensus of the Libraries Management Group was that Draft IV, with some minor modifications, should be adopted.

The project would have concluded at this point, mid-January 1989, if the only intent was to compose an acceptable internal document. The 1989-1993 Long-Range Plan, however, was intended to serve not only as a blueprint for action but also as a public relations vehicle. Copies were slated for distribution to audiences outside the

Library System, such as the university administration, faculty, alumni, donors, corporations and foundations. Unlike an internal document, this long-range plan was obliged to translate complex issues into terms the general public could understand. The next action, taken in Draft V, was to purge the manuscript of unnecessary professional jargon and clarify essential technical terms for the non-librarian reader.

Ready in late February, Draft V was forwarded for external review and comments to the President, the Provost, and the faculty comprising the University Library Committee. Their recommended revisions were incorporated into the definitive text (Draft VI) which was sent to the printer in camera-ready form in late April 1989. At the same time the February draft was being circulated to reviewers, a parallel project was underway to develop a marketing strategy for the plan.

MARKETING THE PLAN

During the preparation of Draft VI, fundamental decisions were made on how to gather internal and external support for the plan. The long-range plan editor was assigned to organize the marketing campaign. This involved preparing an attractive vehicle to carry the Library System's message, developing a suitable special event to announce the plan, and deciding on an appropriate distribution list.

A magazine-style format featuring color photography was selected. The eight weeks between late February and late April were committed to design, photographic reproduction, computer-aided typesetting and final layout, produced entirely in-house through the Library System's Media Services unit. Printed copies of the 1989-1993 Long-Range Plan arrived the first week in June, five weeks after the keylines were submitted to the printer.

The plan was unveiled at a recognition event for Library System employees on June 7, 1989. Shortly thereafter, copies were disseminated to an internal list of all Library System full-time employees, the university leadership, academic and administrative department heads, various Library System advisory groups, library donors, and Library Science Program faculty and alumni leaders.

The publication was also mailed to an external list which included grantmaking foundations headquartered in Michigan, librarians at major local corporations, all ALA-accredited library schools, and selected public, academic and research libraries throughout the country. All told, more than 1,200 copies were distributed within the first month of publication.

Efforts to market the 1989-1993 Long-Range Plan also involved releasing an announcement to the local press, state and national societies, and key professional publications. The notice reported that copies of the plan would be furnished on request for a modest fee.[5] Over the next six months, several dozen libraries responded by requesting copies.

THE PLANNING PROCESS IN RETROSPECT

The entire planning process took sixteen months, if one counts from January 1988 when the planning project was first announced through to the end of April 1989 when the plan in its final form was delivered to the printer. As evidenced in the preceding discussion, the planning period was characterized by four stages: a pre-retreat stage (four months); the two retreats themselves (two months); a post-retreat stage (two months); and the document preparation stage (eight months).

The first eight months through the post-retreat stage were devoted to fact-finding, creative deliberations and preliminary reports using a team approach and various subcommittees. Progress made in the remaining eight months relied on the editor, the Dean and the Associate Dean for leadership and writing services, with the Libraries Management Group and others serving as reviewers.

As much as four months could have been eliminated from the planning process if the following considerations had been handled somewhat differently: (1) developing the background materials; (2) formation of assumptions; (3) defining key results sought; (4) structuring the final document; and (5) organization of the writing process.

1. Developing the background materials. The work groups formed at the end of the May 1988 retreat (Futures, Mission and Objectives, Assumptions, Environment, and Situation) continued to revise their respective reports well into July and in some cases through August. The Futures and Mission and Objectives statements cannot be considered background materials in the strictest sense. Together with the other three work group reports, however, they formed what amounted to "preliminaries." Focusing this much effort on the five reports led the planning team to lose sight of the ultimate goal, to create a concrete statement of what should be done, how and why over the next five years. Since the work group topics were pre-selected by the retreat facilitator rather than developed through committee discussions, this phase of the planning process could have been scheduled prior to the first retreat via "pre-retreat" subcommittees. Any additional refinements needed could have been handled in the two subsequent retreats. This also would have freed time in the post-retreat stage for defining system-wide key results.

2. Formation of assumptions. The wide range of subjects covered by the Assumptions Group suggests that this assignment was of a different order than those performed by the other work groups. The Assumptions Group report combined projections about the future, also found in the Futures and Environment reports, with philosophical statements on values and preferred policies, pertinent to the Mission and Objectives and Situation reports. It might have been more productive to do without an Assumptions Group. As an alternative, the four remaining work groups could have been asked to include a set of starting assumptions in their presentations. An exercise at the second retreat might have served to further delineate relevant assumptions and link them to the all-important key result areas.

3. Defining key results sought. The primary reason for defining key result areas during the second retreat was to prepare for the next step, deciding how the Library System would achieve and evaluate success in those specific areas. Yet no structured process was undertaken in the post-retreat stage for determining the key results sought system-wide. Instead, efforts in July and August focused on work group reports and unit-level key results. A workable plan, defined as action statements with measurable goals, was not reached until Draft IV in mid-January 1989. Rather than dissolve the KRA groups after the June retreat, these subcommittees should have continued to function through the summer. Had they done so, concrete system-wide proposals for collection development, management and access, facilities, information and access services, human resources, external relations, and funding strategies might have been produced by early fall 1988. The development of unit-level key results could have been deferred until a system-wide key results document was available.

4. Structuring the final document. The document preparation stage, which extended from mid-August 1988 through late April 1989, could have been completed in less time if an appropriate structure for the manuscript had been suggested during the retreat or post-retreat stages. The breakthrough came in early December with the decision to use the key result areas as an outline for the document itself. Given that the KRAs were selected during the June retreat, it would have been profitable to have the planning team propose a detailed outline for the publication at that time. Another option would have been to assign a post-retreat task force to investigate how other organizations handled this challenge.[6]

5. Organization of the writing process. Progress on the 1989-1993 Long Range Plan stalled in late summer 1988 when the project was handed over to the editor. Even if the planning team had delivered a workable plan before disbanding in August, the scope of the writing project was too vast to assign to one person. A worthwhile alternative would have been to appoint an editorial team to carry out the next stages in the writing work, organized along the lines of the system-wide key result areas. Draft "chapters" would then be submitted to the editor for further fine tuning and incorporation into the final document.

The long-range planning process can be compared to building a bicycle at the same time you are trying to ride it. The time set aside for participatory decision making, research and writing is time taken away from the more immediate business of running the library. There is also the risk that individual participants or subcommittees may not deliver the best possible product or perform their assignments on schedule. For the Wayne State University Library System, the long-range planning process undertaken in 1988-1989 represented an act of faith in the value of the team approach. Although the process took longer than expected, and possibly longer than necessary, participants were rewarded with a public document that reflects the Library System's aspirations and has carried its message to constituencies around the country.

NOTES

1. By the facilitator's definition, the 1989-1993 Long-Range Plan was actually a strategic plan since a variety of elements were rearranged, added and deleted in the process of its development.

2. According to the Wayne State University Office of Strategic Planning in June 1989, an overall planning document for the university has not yet been attempted. The 850-word University Mission Statement served as the planning team's primary source of guidance on the institution's mission, goals and objectives.

3. Space utilization and physical plant issues, at first listed under Collections, were consolidated later into a sixth Key Result Area entitled "Facilities."

4. The six categories for organizing the background materials became eight sections in the final publication with the separation of "Preservation" from "Collections" and "External Funding" (renamed "Funding Strategies") from "External Relations."

5. Copies of *Wayne State University Libraries Long-Range Plan: 1989-1993* can be obtained at $10 per copy by writing to: Wayne State University Libraries, Office of the Dean, 134 Purdy, Detroit, MI 48202.

6. One publication which could have served as a model is *Choosing a Future for Us and for All of Our Children: The Report of the Detroit Strategic Planning Project*. Detroit: Detroit Renaissance Foundation, November 1987.

Transforming the Library:
Strategic Planning
at Bradley University—
The University Perspective

Martin G. Abegg
Kalman Goldberg

SUMMARY. Strategic planning at Bradley is an institutionalized process, involving common agreement on and commitment to a well-defined mission, with joint participation in developing strategies to achieve the mission's goals. The Library has approached strategic planning as an opportunity to shape both its own future and that of the institution. Based on the University view of the Library as the University's information access center, a strategic vision was developed which focuses on information fluency, rather than hardware. Through a collaborative, iterative process, the vision and the plans to accomplish that vision were developed, refined, disseminated, and widely accepted. Changing technology may invalidate interim strategies, but the vision of the Library at the heart of the academic process will remain a constant and draw support from the entire University community.

Systematic, continuous planning for Bradley University was initiated by the President in 1982. The Provost and Vice President for Academic Affairs was directed to form a Strategic Planning Committee in order to review Bradley's mission statement, to evaluate every academic and support program's relevance and effectiveness toward its achievement, and to develop strategies that would

Martin G. Abegg is President of Bradley University, Peoria, IL. Kalman Goldberg is Provost of Bradley University, Peoria, IL.

131

strengthen these programs. A consultant provided advice on procedures, modified to meet the particular needs of Bradley University. What was to become Phase I of strategic planning began.

The President was motivated by several considerations. Enrollments at the University were declining; although there was no financial crisis, a high level of tuition dependence indicated the likelihood of financial stress in the absence of decisive action; casual observation suggested that some academic programs were no longer appropriate and that there were inefficiencies in some parts of the administrative structure; a major capital campaign was about to be launched and its success depended on both the perception and substantive basis of an academic institution, well managed, worthy of the support of prospective donors.

Bradley has a long tradition of shared governance. No plan or planning process would succeed without the full participation of the University Senate and its faculty, professional staff, administration, and student membership. Consequently, the Strategic Planning Committee, chaired by the Provost, was made a permanent University Senate Committee and is on the permanent agenda of the monthly Senate meetings. The Provost also reports periodically on planning to the Student Senate, even though it has representatives on the University Strategic Planning Committee and the University Senate. The Provost reports on planning to the Academic Affairs Committee of the Board of Trustees and to the full Board at its quarterly meetings. This procedure ensures that the administrative leadership of the University is moving in directions supported by the faculty, staff, students, and Board.

The President and his administrative team understand that the University cannot prosper in the absence of planning; but it also knows that the academy is at its best when faculty are unencumbered by rigid plans, permitting and even encouraging the idiosyncratic and the unpredictable. A contained amount of anarchy is an essential element of a vital university.

Phase I of strategic planning began with a review of the mission statement. The Committee evaluated it in the context of its origin with the founding of Bradley and its historical evolution as Bradley grew and matured; against the background of the existing and evolving socio-economic environment; the spectrum of types of higher education institutions and Bradley's most fruitful position in it in fulfilling its social purpose; and the resource base and potential which determine the limits and the possibilities of how Bradley can function. The Phase II Strategic Planning draft report provides specific, definitive substance to this general statement as it currently applies to Bradley.

With agreement on mission, every academic and support unit was asked to evaluate itself according to two primary criteria: (1) centrality—how vital the program is for the fulfillment of Bradley's mission; (2) quality—how well the unit performs its functions. The Committee decided that all units that were central would be retained. Those of deficient quality were to present a plan for improvement and would receive resources to accomplish it. Units of high quality would be retained even if not highly central. Programs not essential to the mission and of poor quality would be dropped. The Phase I report elaborates on definitions, procedures and specific recommendations. Several programs were dropped; several administrative changes were made; and several new programs were recommended, now prospering. Affected faculty were given special help and ample transition time to find alternative employment and some were able to transfer to other programs within the University.

Of course, the vital centrality of the library is never an issue at a university. But because of its essential role for all programs the burden of high quality is almost uniquely heavy for the library. Evaluation of its performance could only begin with the more obvious criteria of library faculty and staff qualifications and service and depth and breadth of holdings. The actual and potential performance of the library had to be reviewed against a definitive statement of its own mission, viewed in the context of the emerging environment in which Bradley as an institution would be operating as an academic entity in the years ahead. This required a level of imaginative thinking that outpaced the recognized needs of the university units themselves to be served. It was out of this exercise that the concept of the library as the essential information access center emerged, providing the framework for the incorporation of the newest technology, the latest techniques for gathering, storing and providing information in a timely manner, defining the qualifications of library faculty and staff necessary for quality performance, and even setting the stage for the amount and type of new physical facilities required.

Because Phase I was one of critical review, involving retrenchment as well as approbation, it was not accomplished without discord. It was, however, implemented without major disruption or serious damage to morale. The current strength of Bradley is, at least in significant part, attributable to the changes made. The success of Phase I also bears testimony to the importance of a planning process that includes all constituencies, clear explanations of the purposes and processes of the planning exercise, and the opportunity for each affected unit to review, discuss, and respond to recommendations before they become final.

Phase II of strategic planning began in 1987. The University had been strengthened academically and financially. Although declines in the college age pool were projected, separate enrollment management plans and strategies were introduced to ensure stability until the mid-1990's when the trend is expected to reverse. The President convened the Strategic Planning Committee with the following charge, shared subsequently with the University Senate and Board of Trustees for their assent and with all faculty and staff in a memorandum for their information and support.

> Bradley University is on the threshold of becoming a nationally recognized comprehensive university of very high quality. In order to achieve this promise we must:
>
> 1. configure each of the academic and support programs for five to ten years hence in imaginative but realistic terms as we attempt to become a "model" institution of our type. This would include: the academic programs; the range of pedagogies suited to each; the ways in which modern technology can be integrated into curricula; the student body size and structure (male/female, geographic distribution, ethnic composition, socioeconomic compo-

sition, academic/talent mix); support program; the faculty and professional staff needs; capital needs;

2. recognize that at a stable optimum size, the University cannot be self-supporting from tuition income. Consequently, the Committee should estimate the cost of operating Bradley University as envisaged, keeping within a realistic growth figure for both unrestricted giving and endowment earning for generating the additional income.

Other committees external to the University will be formed as part of the planning process to work with this Academic Committee. The academic programs will drive the plan, the other committees will provide information and realistic estimates of the constraints within which we must plan.

The purposes of Phase I and the planning underway during this period of national enrollment pool decline were to achieve consensus on Bradley's mission and the academic programs central to its fulfillment. An additional, concomitant planning program serves as a bridge between Phase I and Phase II. With the resources available from tuition and growing gifts we are positioning the University for quality growth in the 1990's, setting the stage for Phase II. Phase I posed a threat to many programs; Phase II offers promise of fulfillment of their academic aspirations. The outline of the Phase II draft report suggests the overall vision for Bradley's future, the role each of the units, with the Committee's approval, intends to play in its achievement. Each academic and support unit has its unique contribution, but all are committed to the fulfillment of Bradley's mission in ways that are relevant for the next decade or more.

The Phase II report will be reviewed by other task forces, some external to the campus. These groups will be represented on the President's Committee which, with the Development Office, will launch the next capital campaign. Informed and driven by the academic plan of the Strategic Planning Committee, a fund drive to increase the endowment will be undertaken. The income from the expanded endowment will provide the supplement to tuition income and annual gifts required to make the fulfillment of the academic plan and Bradley's mission possible.

Planning has become institutionalized at Bradley. There is common agreement on and commitment to a well-defined mission. The tradition of shared responsibility for the governance of the University ensures joint participation in developing strategies to achieve the mission's goals. The success Bradley is enjoying in elevating its quality, spreading its reputation beyond its own region, completing a capital funds drive, and establishing fiscal stability is seen as a consequence of planning, reinforcing the effort.

Transforming the Library:
Strategic Planning
at Bradley University —
The Library Perspective

Ellen I. Watson

OVERVIEW

Cullom-Davis Library, as part of the Bradley University Information Technologies and Resources unit, approached strategic planning as an opportunity to shape both its own future and that of the institution. The Library both leads and follows. We lead by establishing architectures, fundamental information management and movement capabilities, and by providing both the training for and examples of new information strategies. We follow in the sense that we adapt our plans to the present and future needs of the University's academic and administrative programs. The focus of both current activities and strategic planning is on information fluency, rather than on hardware.

The University — administration, faculty, and the Library itself — views the Library as the University's information access center. The Library provides the basic collections and resources needed for the University's teaching and research activities, and enhances those collections with access to the expanding universe of information resources of all types and formats. This view of the Library was central to the strategic planning process and to the strategic vision of the Library as it developed.

The Library's role in the strategic planning process of the Univer-

Ellen I. Watson is Director of Cullom-Davis Library, Bradley University, Peoria, IL.

137

sity has been influenced by its administrative reporting structure. Prior to 1986, the Library was an autonomous service reporting to the office of the Provost. Bradley's information management units—including the Library as the University's information access center—were reorganized as Information Technologies and Resources in 1986. Included within this unit are the Cullom-Davis Library, Computing Services, the Center for Learning Resources, and Telecommunications (see Table 1).

This organizational structure has worked well for the University: the approach and organizational model spans all appropriate technologies and resources. The organizational structure has worked equally well for the Library, ensuring that the Library's needs are included in all university-wide planning for information resources and services, allowing coordination with other information providers, and encouraging the development of a new vision of Library programs and roles. The Library has taken a leadership role within Information Technologies, promoting and defining information fluency. As part of this process, the Library is expanding and enhanc-

TABLE 1

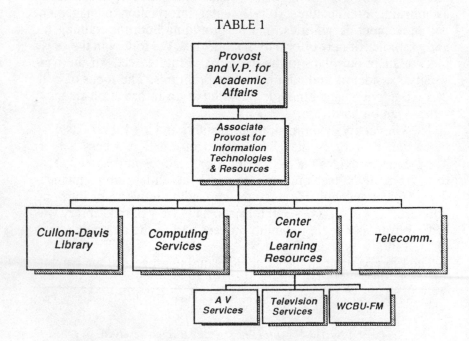

ing programs to become the end-user's primary contact point for information services and delivery.

The University's strategic planning process occurred at a propitious time for the Information Technologies and Resources unit in general, and for the Library in particular. Information Technologies had undertaken no unit-wide planning of its own since its inception, and the Library was in the process of planning for a building expansion and renovation, as well as installing a new director. These events presented both challenges and opportunities: they forced us to define mission and functions, and provided mechanisms for a direct translation of visions into concrete-and-steel, as well as more fluid forms. The cooperation required to develop a strategic plan also helped Information Technologies managers gain a broader perspective of the roles of each of the components, and envision some new ways in which the components might interact in support of each other. The Library also seized on strategic planning as an opportunity to be proactive — to place the Library's plans and agenda within the overall institutional plan — as well as to develop programs and services in response to expressed needs.

PROCESS

One of the most important components of the planning process was the inclusion — the centrality — of a strategic vision as the motivating factor in each academic and administrative unit's strategic plan. In the Library, this strategic vision became the standard against which current status and future goals were measured. In many cases, we worked backward from the vision to develop the outline of operational plans to realize that vision.

Because this was the first planning effort since the establishment of Information Technologies and Resources and the University's commitment to aggressively implement information technologies throughout the institution, we supplemented the University's strategic planning outline with elements drawn from standard strategic planning methodology. The development of the Information Technologies plan was based on an iterative model. Unit managers developed drafts which were reviewed by the Information Technologies Executive Committee, followed by further revision and review, and extensive collaboration. The process, while offering each unit manager the opportunity to substantially affect the final product, was not wholly successful. The Library Director was the most active of the unit managers throughout the process, having more impact on the final plan than any other manager. The process also included attempts to iteratively plan with other administrative and academic units. While these efforts were only marginally successful, the dissemination of the Information Technologies plan early in the process did result in a wide acceptance of the Information Technologies vision — and especially that of the Library — and the inclusion of many elements of that vision in the plans of other academic and administrative units.

Several factors affected the Library's participation in the planning process, and in the plan as it developed. In the design of the strategic planning process and the development of the University's academic strategies, Library participation occurred through the Associate Provost for Information Technologies and Resources. The Associate Provost used the meetings of the Information Technologies Executive Committee and meetings with the Library Director and Library staff as sources for the concerns and issues he relayed to the University Strategic Planning Committee.

At the time the strategic planning process began, the Library was without a permanent director and was planning an expansion to nearly double the size of the physical facility. This meant that much of the collective professional energy of the Library staff and administration was inwardly directed, rather than focused on university-wide issues and perspectives. It also meant, however, that the Library was in the midst of a major project that both required and facilitated long-range vision and planning for the physical plant and for services — an ideal situation in which to develop a strategic vision and to take immediate, dramatic action to ensure that many of the physical requirements necessary to support that vision could be accommodated.

In part because of the pressures of the building project and the change in Library administration, no Library Strategic Planning Committee was formed. Instead, first drafts of the mission, status and goals were developed by the Acting Library Director, and reviewed with Library faculty. That essential material was then further reviewed and substantially revised and expanded by the new Director. Library faculty reviewed the strategic vision, goals, and implementation strategies repeatedly over a four-month period, adding new refinements and definition to the plans and assuring a library-wide understanding of and commitment to the vision as it developed. As the document began to take final shape, it was reviewed by the full staff, and served as the basis for discussion at a full staff meeting. The strategic plan began as an individual vision, but became, through the review and revision process, a communal model.

Throughout its development, the strategic plan was criticized, evaluated, and refined through comparison and discussion with other Information Technologies managers, the Associate Provost, and academic units throughout the institution. The vision of the Library as the primary information access point for the University was accepted as an Information Technologies focus through this review process. The Associate Provost provided ongoing input and feedback during the process, ensuring that the plan retained its focus, that conflicting ideas and expectations among managers were resolved, and that the document remained coherent, readable, and even lively.

External review of the Library's plan was provided by the University Library Committee, an *ad hoc* advisory committee appointed by the Provost. The University Library Committee has faculty representation from each of the University's colleges, administrative representation from the Graduate School and Continuing Education, and undergraduate and graduate student representation. University Library Committee members read and critiqued various drafts of the Library's strategic plan.

The final report, "Information Technologies and Resources: Strategic Planning Report," was submitted to the University Strategic Planning Committee in November, 1988. A two volume document, with approximately 135 pages of narrative in the first volume, and an appendix of data of approximately 75 pages in the second volume, the full report was carefully and critically reviewed by a subcommittee of the University Strategic Planning Committee. This subcommittee raised questions of substance, including the new role for the Library, interaction between existing "traditional" services and resources in the Library and the envisioned electronic technologies and services, and the costs of the proposed new directions.

The penultimate stage in the planning process was the development of a summary document which condensed the full plan's strategic vision into approximately 35 pages. The summary went through several iterations before taking its final form in November of 1989. While the distillation was a painful process, in the end it was a productive one: the final summary is more than a condensation of the original report. Its brevity has sharpened the vision, and highlighted the relationships between the unit components. The guidance provided by the draft outline for the University report indicated areas in which Information Technologies can additionally support academic units. The requirement that we prioritize for the University Strategic Planning Committee our visions, goals and objectives has forced us to focus on the overall good, rather than protecting our individual units' turf. The final document will be of ongoing value to Information Technologies and Resources, and to the Library in particular.

Strategic planning at Bradley, especially the strategic planning of the Library, has been based upon a future vision of the University. The following statement of that future vision has been excerpted from the Executive Summary of the Information Technologies Strategic Planning Report. The excerpt is written from the vantage point of 1997, the University's centenary year, looking backward to the accomplishments of the previous years—the results of the implementation of the strategic plan.

STRATEGIC VISION: 1997

The Library of Bradley's centenary year stands at the heart of the academic life of the University, providing services that stimulate the entire academic process. The traditional functions and services of an academic library are still very evident. However, these are interpreted and provided in new ways, with an emphasis on personal service to meet the expanded information needs of the University Community.

The Library is physically similar to the Library of 1990;

however, the shelves are more nearly full and the space fully occupied. The facility still looks and feels like a "library" — filled with print-on-paper materials, study spaces and meeting rooms, with fully staffed access desks. The Library has maintained its "high touch" environment in the midst of "high tech" innovation.

Today's users find that the Library has adapted technology to provide increased personalization and a broader range of services to information seekers. Networking options offer direct access to a vast international pool of information resources, while the assistance of knowledgeable librarians is available to facilitate that access. Technology has been applied in subtle ways, so as to enhance and assist the work of scholars, rather than simply replacing books with electronics.

An expert system shell named BRUTIS (BRadley University Total Information System) guides the user to needed materials within the collections. BRUTIS allows users to approach information searches at their individual level of expertise, prompting the novice and rapidly executing the requests of the expert. Through this window, local and distant databases, indices, full-text and graphics retrieval, personal materials orders, and numerous other services are available.

An integrated Administrative Information Support System (AISS), offered through the Library with resources from other Information Technologies units, provides senior administration with information and research data in support of planning and decision making.

The Library's conferences and exhibits have attracted such a wide following that the sessions are often filled to capacity and the discussions spill over into cafeterias, residence halls, and classrooms.

Designated by the State as a Regional Conservation Center, the Library has not only successfully arrested the physical deterioration of its own collections, but, through an innovative marriage of technology and tradition, developed a preservation program which has attracted attention throughout the Midwest.

Staffing patterns have changed in response to the Library's

expanded functions. Bibliographic instruction and reference services are provided on-demand via electronic referrals and are conducted interactively over the computer network. To accommodate this demand, librarians and other information professionals provide service approximately 18 hours per day, often from locations other than the Library itself. Librarians have been joined by other information professionals, including experts in computer networking and artificial intelligence, who share joint appointments in the Library and Computing Services.

Although there have been dramatic changes in the Library, the essential nature and mission of the Library remain as stated in 1989: support of the educational process at Bradley University. The Library is an active agent in effecting positive changes in that process, enhancing Bradley's visibility and reputation as a leading academic institution.

PRODUCT

At several points during the strategic planning process—especially in the midst of construction debris and pressing issues of access to our collections and study space—we asked ourselves, "Is it worth it?" Our answer is, emphatically, "Yes."

While the final report of the University Strategic Planning Committee is still being written, preliminary information indicates that Information Technologies and the Library will figure prominently in the University's strategic vision. The Information Technologies plan has shaped the institutional plan: it has maintained Information Technologies in its values and momentums, established new capabilities and goals, and formalized the strategic role of information technologies. The Information Technologies plan and process has also created a forum for effective collaboration with all segments of the institution, resulting in improved articulation and increased internalization of information technologies by those units.

The Library's essential role in support of quality academic programs and high quality, highly productive faculty has been stressed by each of the academic units. The Library's own vision of how this support can be provided—through both traditional and innovative formats and services — seems to be well accepted. With an increasing institutional emphasis on the cultural and intellectual life of the University community, the Library's proposals to increase its role and visibility in these areas have been well received. The final report will accept and validate the Library's role as the University's central information resource.

Some of the proposals which we expect to be included in the final report are already being implemented. As part of the Library's new role as information access center, an extensive array of networked microcomputer workstations have been placed in the Library, and a member of the User Services staff of Computing Services has an office in the Library to provide training and support for electronic information activities. A series of lectures, performances, and exhibits are planned to begin with the dedication of the new facility and extend into the Library's future. Collection development — including assessment, priorities, and funding options — is underway to ensure that the collection, whatever its formats and media, meets curricular and faculty needs. Current implementation is based upon allocations through the normal University budgeting process. Implementation of the remaining vision will depend upon additional external as well as internal funding sources, together with substantial administrative collaboration within Information Technologies.

The most important product of the strategic planning process was not the document produced, but the shared vision that was developed. This sharing occurred within the Library and its staff and advisory structure, within the Information Technologies and Resources unit as a whole, and in external sharing of the vision with the institution. Changing technology may well invalidate interim strategies, but the vision of the Library at the heart of the academic process, providing information access and promoting information literacy to all University constituents, will remain a constant and draw support from all of the University community.

Conformity and Diversity:
Local Library Planning
in a Multi-Campus System

Russell Shank

SUMMARY. The current era of planning for library service in the University of California began in the mid-1970s with the development of the Universitywide plan. Although the organization and academic programs of each of the nine campuses are independently administered by campus chancellors, the libraries are centrally budgeted. Library planning at UCLA to match campus-specific needs has required, therefore, the creation of a sophisticated complex of committees, task groups and external organizational relationships for various staff members. Planning is a primary continuing function of the administration of the Library.

THE GENERAL SETTING

The University of California is owned, in essence, and operated by a Board of Regents, created by the Constitution of the State of California. Constitutionally, the University of California is the only publicly funded institution of higher education in the state authorized to offer the PhD degree. The University has nine campuses administered by Chancellors who are responsible to the Board of Regents through the President of the University. The Chancellors may organize their campus operations to suit their visions and styles. They are bound only by general policies of the Regents. Academic programs are subject to approval by the faculties through the operation of the Academic Senate which has divisions on each campus, with, of course, final certification by the President and the

---

Russell Shank is Assistant Vice Chancellor for Library and Information Services Planning, University of California at Los Angeles.

147

Regents of the University. The Regents have ultimate authority for operation of the University, without veto by the Governor or Legislature, except through special "enabling" legislation for specific purposes. To the maximum extent possible, the Regents and the President allow the Chancellors to administer their campuses as independently as can be justified.

Given this freedom, the Chancellors have various organizational arrangements that affect their libraries. Many campuses have Academic Vice Chancellors to whom the libraries report. The UCLA organization has a Vice Chancellor for Academic Administration who is responsible for the Library, the art galleries, the media centers, the Television and Film Archive, and similar units. The University Librarians on each campus are members of the Academic Senate by virtue of their positions. The nine University Librarians are members of a systemwide Library Council, chaired by the University's Senior Vice President for Academic Affairs. The Chancellors meet regularly as a Council of Chancellors. Other groups of peers in operational functions among the campuses also meet from time to time to exchange information and to prepare reports which may lead to policy statements for the University as a whole.

This only begins to describe the organization for control, administration and communication in the University as a system. For planning purposes the administrators of campus departments must be sensitive to the powers of these agents, the timing for the communication among them, and the status of guidelines under deliberation or forthcoming from them.

One of the key functions of the University Librarian at UCLA has been to lead the staff into an understanding of the meaning of the work of these agents which is essential for planning purposes. This has been accomplished through the assignment of administrative staff members to work on various committees and task groups throughout the University whenever this can be arranged, the creation of committees in the Library with interlocking memberships, including the appropriate administrative staff members, the establishment of a series of regular and special meetings of these groups as is required to feed information into the Library's organization, and a calendar of times for the presentation of data and information to the staff and other University administrators.

PLANNING

The planning system used by the UCLA Library is that proposed by George Steiner, a specialist in planning from the UCLA Graduate School of Management.[1] In Steiner's view, planning may be defined in at least four ways. First, long-range planning is "the systematic identification of opportunities and threats that lie in the future which, in combination with other relevant data, provide a basis for management to make current decisions to exploit the opportunities and to avoid the threats."[2] Second, strategic planning is a continuous process of "deciding in advance what is to be done, when it is to be done, how it is to be done, and who is going to do it."[3] Third, it is a philosophy. It "is more of a thought process, an intellectual exercise, than a prescribed set of processes, procedures, structures or techniques."[4] Fourth, it is a comprehensive and flexible "structure of plans that integrates strategic with short-range operational plans,"[5] and takes into account objectives, strategies and policies at all levels of an organization. Making forecasts of the internal and external environment is an essential early task in planning. Strategic planning is not, however, the making of future decisions. Planning is best if it maximizes an agency's ability to meet successfully its customers' expectations as environmental conditions change. The success of forecasting, therefore, is best measured in terms of the agency's position as things change, rather than whether the forecast proves to be accurate.

Formal planning has taken place at several levels in the University in recent years. These efforts feed each other, or interact to provide guidelines for planning and decisions at succeeding lower levels in the hierarchy. One becomes the background for checking the utility and feasibility of another.

Planning for local campus library service in the University of California, however, is fraught with an additional complication. While each campus plans its academic operations independently (with ultimate action for general academic programs subject to approval by the University's Board of Regents), the nine campuses' libraries' policies are directed by the central University administration as if the libraries were an "overlay" on the campuses, provided by the central administration. Library service is the only campus-directed function of the University that is so administered. It is budgeted separately from the campuses by systemwide officials. The library administrators on each of the nine campuses must use their ingenuity in allocating the general funds appropriated to the campuses for library functions, or in raising or tapping other funding, to operate and meet local needs. This heightens the need for careful planning.

The current era of planning for library service throughout the University of California began in the mid-1970s. The University administration at that time decided it would not request funds for growth of the libraries of the nine campuses until a plan had been laid out for their coordinated development. This was deemed a prudent move by the administration in dealing with the Governor and the legislature of the State. The position of Executive Director of Universitywide Planning was created at the central University administrative level to direct the creation of this plan and to guide its implementation.

The principle agent for deliberation on the organization and content to the plan was the Library Council, composed of the University Librarians of the nine campuses, the deans of the University's two library schools, several members of the faculty of the University, and the Executive Director of Universitywide Library Planning. There were, in addition, other important groups in the University's organization with strong interests in the libraries' programs: the Academic Senate, with legislative assemblies on each campus, the Council of Chancellors of the campuses, and several other groupings of peers in the administration. Drafts of the developing plan were shared with all of these groups for their consideration and comment.

The plan that evolved was, in the main, the work of the Executive Director of Universitywide Planning. Although its several drafts were thoroughly reviewed and discussed by various groups its main goals never varied: (a) the nine campus libraries were to operate as if they were one university library; (b) there would be a common, nine-campus automation program; (c) acquisitions budgets would be increased and allocated among the campuses according to a formula based on academic programs; and (d) the ever-growing collections would be housed through a combination of a limited amount of campus space growth and the addition of two regional cooperative shelving facilities.

Iterations of the developing plan were largely refinements of proposed operations and additions of policy and definitions within these general initiatives. Although there continued to be questions, action could not be delayed in the face of continued restricted funding, and the plan was adopted in 1977[6] (hereafter referred to as the *UC Plan for Library Development*, the systemwide *Plan* or just the *Plan*) with the understanding that arguments on details would be considered and adjudicated through continued planning effort.

The *Plan* was at least two years in the making, and went through four iterations. It created what became a contractual document between the legislature and the University, which provided specific directions for development and financial growth of the libraries. It was augmented once in subsequent years to take into account one aspect of library need that had been overlooked. Otherwise it has been unaltered in nearly 15 years. No funds are sought for any particular library activity on a specific campus: all funding is argued in terms of the systemwide *Plan*. The Library Council must agree on priorities each year within the boundaries of the *Plan*, regardless of variations in local needs.

The UCLA Library's criticism of this planning effort, following Steiner's analysis, is based on the fact that it was not continuous. There was a call for comments about needs for adjustments in the *Plan* after one year, but comments were either ignored or explained away. A second approach to revision of the *Plan* seven years later was ignored even though it resulted in a carefully crafted plan for new deliberations with assignments of responsibilities and a time scale for completion.

Planning at the campus level, therefore, for the development of local library service has taken on heightened significance. Nothing constrains the operation of such a planning function: the subsequent local activities are, however, bound by the policies and funding provided by the *Plan*. Success in local decision-making requires the creation of coalitions with other campus departments involved in the management of information resources and the provision of information access services, or the raising of private funds.

On the UCLA campus planning takes place at many levels and in many sectors of campus operations. The probability of success of the Library's planning effort, or at least of the selection of appropriate strategies and tactics to guide the Library's actions, varies directly with the ability of the decision-makers in the Library to tap the flow of information within these other sectors. The task for local library management has been to determine actions at the local level that are vital to the development and innovation of successful information services, and to define them to conform to the higher plan, to find alternatives that fall outside the scope of the *UC Plan for Library Development*, or to defend any lack of timely action in terms that do not demean the systemwide *Plan*.

Almost simultaneously with the publication of the *UC Plan for Library Development*, the UCLA Library was reorganized to ensure (a) the effective monitoring of the environment in which the library operated, and (b) the deliberation on issues by those who were expected to be able to identify them, to develop alternatives for their resolution, and to implement and monitor selected courses of action. This was achieved through the creation of an Executive Committee (EXCOM) comprised of the University Librarian and the Assistant and Associate University Librarians, an Administrative Conference (ADCON) comprised of EXCOM and the Library's unit heads (later changed to include only those unit heads who reported to EXCOM members), and as many librarywide task groups and advisory committees as were required to enhance cooperative work on projects and issues of concern to the Library in general.

"Interlocking directorates" were created by having various members of EXCOM serve on committees and task forces of the University's Library Council, and on UCLA Library committees. The Library was tied to the campuses' academic program through the membership of the University Librarian in the Academic Senate, by virtue of which he served from time to time on the Senate's Planning Committee. He also served on the UCLA Academic Affairs Council and the UCLA Committee on Capital and Space Planning—key agents in campus planning. In addition each member of EXCOM was made responsible for establishing working relationships with key campus administrators important to the functioning of their jobs.

Four times in a dozen years, the Library administration has held "retreats" for various groups in the Library to establish the ground-work for administrative guidance and staff understanding of the development of library service, either in general or on specific, though long-range, issues. Among the latter were the need to retrench in the face of tax-cutting programs in the State, and the future of the card catalog. A brief study of retreats cited several recommendations, one of which was quite accurate—namely that retreats have been useful in large and complex libraries as a method of staff and organizational development.[7] In the more general retreats the group used the Steiner WOTS UP approach to deliberations on future actions whereby the focus was first on goals, and then on Library weakness, and opportunities, and threats to its development and its strengths.[8] In at least one of the retreats, the nominal group technique was used to establish consensus on priorities.

The monitoring of the implementation of elements of plans, their modification and updating have been major tasks. EXCOM has met once a year in mini-retreats to determine the best allocation of funds for the year. ADCON has met on a varying schedule, but monthly as much as possible. Each member of EXCOM has had regular meetings with unit heads reporting to them. In the past year, EXCOM and ADCON have made strong moves to prepare annual planning and goal statements. And EXCOM has met annually with the Library's unit heads to conduct executive reviews, examining achievements, goals, objectives, and the need for resources. In this way, the Library has moved along the various paths suggested by Steiner, tracking the environment, discussing the implications of the plans of other units in the University which are seemingly related to the Library's functions, making modifications in the Library's plans, and trying to determine when a major reexamination of the Library's plans seems to be required.

Currently the chief influence on thinking about the directions of the UCLA Library is the result of the Chancellor's strategic planning program. This program began in December 1986 with the appointment of a Strategic Planning Committee composed of sixteen faculty members charged with the tasks of setting UCLA's mission and with identifying the issues that would have significant impact on UCLA's ability to enter the twenty-first century. The Committee appointed ten task forces to examine such issues as the need for faculty renewal, the quality of campus life, and the University and the community. Late in its work the Committee appointed an additional task force specifically to focus on library issues.

The Committee's report was issued in late 1989, and has become the center of attention of a second effort to consider what must be done to achieve the goals of the plan. Some of the recommendations in the report can be implemented immediately; some will require further discussion. Further, the recommendations are generally quite broad and general, leaving considerable room for strategic moves that will achieve goals. And, of course, decisions affecting the Library system must take into account the environment created by the 1977 *UC Plan for Library Development*.

These are issues that will be considered by a newly created position of Assistant Vice Chancellor for Library and Information Services Planning. There is no reason to believe that the style of planning effort just described need be changed in this new era. Indeed, the growing complexity of the organization of campus information resource management will require more communication and assessment of the environment by more parties than ever. If anything changes, it will most likely be that decisions on allocation of resources by the campus administration will be more complicated, and will require more sophisticated methods for their implementation.

COMMENTS

The existence of a formal planning process does not guarantee the identification of the exact decisions that have to be made. Broad involvement in the planning effort by many groups both creates opportunities for many vested interests to have voices in the goals and content of the plan, and for vexatious confrontations and complications arising from the timing of the communication of questions, opinions and advice. Committees or task groups with assignments in the planning function are, nevertheless essential to the process. They increase the probability of the identification of useful information, ideas, and opinions. No matter how carefully constructed they are, however, they do not guarantee unanimity of view, understanding or capability. Nor do they necessarily achieve consensus. The meaning of facts can be disputed. They deal chiefly with words and arguments: those who command rhetoric may fare well. There will still be times when the head of the library system will have to make what seem to be intuitive decisions. Acceptance of planning depends in large measure on the credibility of the decision-maker. Planning, however, should raise the probability that operational decisions will be appropriate to local conditions.

Groupings of peers in functional or organizational roles can be useful even if they are not considered part of the planning process, chiefly through their exposition of environmental conditions — tracking, as it is sometimes called. At UCLA they have provided the mechanism for continual monitoring of the implementation of decisions based on long-range planning, and the modification of activities to overcome hitches in implementation.

Properly done, formal planning, including the work that has to be done by all managers in an organization which assumes that planning is a major function of management, is time-consuming. It requires a style of administration that encourages deliberation, values opinions, displays faith in the work of others, rewards risk-taking, and recognizes the difference between varying but valid decisions and mistaken judgements.

NOTES

1. George Albert Steiner, *Management Policy and Strategy* (New York: Macmillan Publishing Co., 1986).
2. Ibid., p.81.
3. Ibid. (The same page as the preceding note.)
4. Ibid. (The same page as Note 2.)
5. Ibid. (The same page as Note 2).
6. *The University of California Libraries: A Plan for Development, 1978-1988* (Berkeley, California, University of California, Office of the Executive Director of Universitywide Library Planning, 1977).
7. E. Dale Cluff and Gisela Webb, "Staff Retreats in ACRL Libraries," *College and Research Library News* 49(1988): 521.
8. Steiner, *Management Strategy and Policy*, 86.

BIBLIOGRAPHY

Cathcart, Jim. How to Conduct a Strategic Planning Retreat. *Training and Development Journal* (May 1986):63-65.

Cluff, E. Dale and Webb, Gisela. Staff Retreats in ACRL Libraries. *College and Research Library News* 49(1988):517-521.

Espy, Siri N. *Handbook of Strategic Planning for Nonprofit Organizations*. New York: Praeger, 1986.

Morrison, James L. *Futures Research and the Strategic Planning Process: Implications for Higher Education*. Washington, D.C.: Association for the Study of Higher Education, 1984.

Office of the Executive Director of Universitywide Library Planning. *The University of California Libraries: a Plan for Development*. Berkeley, California: University of California, 1977.

Steiner, George Albert. *Management Policy and Strategy*. New York: Macmillan, 1986.

Planning for Diversity: Strategic Planning for an Urban Academic Library

Marilyn Mitchell
Rutherford W. Witthus

SUMMARY. The Auraria Library, a multi-institutional urban academic library in Denver, Colorado, approached the strategic planning process with the assumption that urban academic institutions and their libraries differ from their traditional counterparts. This paper defines urbanism and examines the organization values audit and the environmental scan as crucial elements of the strategic planning process in an urban context.

Planning in libraries is not new. Public and academic libraries have acknowledged the value of short- and long-range planning explicitly since World War II and implicitly for many years before that. As libraries have become involved in and have experienced the results of their planning efforts they have turned increasingly to the strategic planning model as developed in the corporate and governmental setting. This strategic model is generally understood to mean a process in which options are identified and evaluated in the context of the organization's shared values as articulated in its mission statement, the external environment in which it operates, and the resources required to achieve its goals. As libraries are usually not independently funded and administered agencies but rather serve as parts of larger academic, municipal or corporate structures,

Marilyn Mitchell is Assistant Director for Collection and Automation Services at Auraria Library, University of Colorado at Denver, CO. Rutherford W. Witthus is Head of Archives and Special Collections at Auraria Library, University of Colorado at Denver, CO.

the strategic planning applied in the library setting relies heavily on an understanding of the essential qualities of the parent institution, its mission, clientele, stakeholders, size and location.

The authors of this article participated in a strategic planning process for the Auraria Library, a multi-institutional urban academic library. This process is yet to be completed as the article goes to press. The Auraria Library is administered by the University of Colorado at Denver and serves that institution as well as Metropolitan State College and the Community College of Denver. All three institutions share a single campus and set of facilities, including the library, which has been in operation since 1976. The three institutions maintain separate identities through their individual missions. The library developed a mission statement ten years ago which tried to address the academic needs of the three institutions as well as those of the urban community. However, administrators in all three institutions have changed a number of times bringing new interpretations to their various mission statements and it became clear that the library did not, in fact, have a mission statement that defined its purpose under the changing campus conditions. It was determined that strategic planning was necessary to clarify the mission of the library and to identify the constituencies to be served.

The Auraria campus is considerably more complex academically, administratively, and politically than the usual urban academic institution and, in many respects, the Auraria Library is a unique expression of library service. This paper will not delve into the complexities of the situation but mentions it only as the context for a more theoretical examination of the strategic planning process in an urban academic library. For irrespective of the specifics of the situation, developing a working application of the model required considerable thinking about the relationship between urban academic institutions and their libraries and understanding the actual role of the values audit and the environmental scan in the process. Our assumptions in undertaking strategic planning were that urban academic institutions and their libraries do differ in significant ways from their traditional counterparts. Therefore, one would expect significant differences in both the planning process and the interpretation of the data generated in that process. This paper presents the conceptual framework of these assumptions.

URBANISM AND THE URBAN
ACADEMIC LIBRARY

To understand what makes an urban academic library different from other academic libraries requires an overview of the various meanings of *urbanism*. No one definition will account for the richness and diversity of the concept.

Opposite of rural is not a satisfactory definition, yet it does bring us closer to understanding something about urbanism. The common image of rural life usually includes a sense of a quiet, focused time. Many chores are completed during the course of a day, yet each task appears to have a beginning and an end. Each person seems to know what to do and when to do it. Changes in the weather or of the seasons constitute significant change. People-induced change, when it happens, happens slowly. This idealized image, of course, does not always match the reality of the rural life.

When we compare this image to that of an urban area, we see that *opposite of rural* does, in fact, clarify the concept of urbanism. An urban environment is characterized by diversity—diverse people, diverse activities, diverse schedules, diverse locations, and diverse goals. Changes, sometimes rapid and continuous, are common enough to be ignored. Urban areas change because people both allow and encourage technology to advance. Sociologist Jerome Krase describes the ideal city as "the most modern environment in which change and diversity in all aspects of life are accepted if not fostered."[1] New York City librarian Barbara Dunlap reports that living in a city "is living in a world of multiple yet insufficient resources, a world filled with opportunities, uncertainty and lack of time."[2]

An urban academic library is an academic library situated in a technologically advanced, changing environment characterized by a diversity of people, resources, and services. And from that environment the library draws its clientele, its workers, and its support. The library is not alone in this respect. Its parent institution, the urban academic college or university, possesses many of the same defining characteristics.

The most important difference between the urban and the traditional institution is the degree to which the urban institution merges with and interacts with its urban environment. The city is the classroom and the classroom is often the city in microcosm. Internships and other forms of cooperative education provide learning experiences. Many urban professors also work in the corporate, professional, or governmental sectors of the community. Some are even loaned to the institution to bring a community perspective to the classroom. Their research is often more applied than theoretical. Their funding often comes from the community they are serving. Whether funded or not, they are often more involved in providing direct service to the urban or corporate society surrounding the campus. In essence, the urban institution is less self-contained. The ivory tower is replaced by a semipermeable membrane. The academic life is not a retreat from temporal life, but rather an integral part of it.

Understanding the diversity and change that characterize the environment of an urban academic institution does not guarantee that the planning process will be imbued with the knowledge of how to maximize the richness of urbanism's inherent diversity and change. R. B. Heydinger observed that colleges and universities have evolved through four stages of planning: budget planning, goal and objective setting, forecasting, and strategic planning."[3] This last, strategic planning, requires that planners discover the richness or paucity of the environment in which their stakeholders, their competitors, and their own institutions operate and plan for the future. However, a successful future depends on continuing the strategic planning process by transforming its players into strategic thinkers.

Just as an urban institution differs from its more traditional counterpart, so does the planning process differ. In discussing these differences, it must be pointed out that they are not absolutes but differences of degree on a continuum. Thus, everything which is stated about the urban context can also be said for the traditional context. However, there is always a difference of degree — important in itself and important cumulatively as it defines the urban experience. Specific differences encountered when applying any strategic planning model to an urban institution are found in the processes surrounding the values audit, the mission statement, and the environmental scan.

THE VALUES AUDIT
AND THE MISSION STATEMENT

The values audit attempts to uncover and articulate the subjective feelings held about the organization by members of the organization. It can serve to identify attitudes toward the mission, the goals, the services, and the clientele. Likewise it can define the organization's ideology or style, its orientation to power, roles, tasks, or individuals. And it can identify the behavioral norms of its employees, how they perform as individuals or collectively.

Determining what it is that the library does and how it gets it done is crucial to understanding its *de facto* mission as well as determining what its mission ought to be. That higher education and academic libraries have changed and continue to change is axiomatic. The library in the urban institution is in the forcfront of this change. Most library staff and faculty, and students, as well, understand traditional education and traditional library services in support of that education. Most were educated in that system and received those services. Urban education is, in many respects, synonymous with non-traditional education, universities without walls, weekend colleges, free universities, open enrollments, and class schedules to meet the time constraints of working students. Urban academic libraries, like academic libraries everywhere, have met the needs of these non-traditional students through bibliographic instruction geared towards lifelong learning and electronic access to specific information.

But urban libraries have been asked to take an additional step of meeting the information and instructional needs of constituents who may not be formally affiliated with the institution. They are simply a part of the larger urban community served by the campus in other ways. They may be constituents drawn to the library through a number of cooperative arrangements which typically link the campus library with a network of public and special libraries in the metropolitan area.

The values audit may uncover a very conflicted organization as staff struggle with what is, what ought to be, or what might be. The staff not only must interact with the various constituencies; they are, themselves, part of those constituencies. Any mission statement, to be understood and championed by the staff, must reflect their own feelings of the value of the organization. Before the library can draft a mission statement, all these unstated assumptions and value judgements of the proper role of the library must be uncovered, articulated, and prioritized.

The library's mission statement must reflect the values and parallel the mission of the parent institution. Likewise, the parent institution must reflect the values of the community of which it is a part. Urban institutions often give considerable lip service to outreach and service to the community with very little policy guidance on how these nonaffiliates shall, in fact, be served. For urban library staff, this may be a very real struggle, made manifest during every open hour.

The values audit will reveal many differences within the library and possibly between the library, the parent institution, and the community. Strategic planning must address these differences before proceeding to the formulation of a mission statement.

CONTINUOUS ENVIRONMENTAL SCANNING

Environmental scanning is not just a source of date on the external world. For an urban academic library, whose mission merges directly with the needs of the urban community, scanning is the way to maintain awareness of the community in which the library and its parent institution find themselves. In addition, it provides that back drop against which internal values may be clarified. Finally, environmental scanning serves to position the library within the mission of the parent institution.

The external factors usually monitored during environmental scanning include economic conditions and probable economic development, all levels of policy decisions and political attitudes likely to affect the institution, demographic information and projections reflecting the community's social structure, and the extent of technological progress in the community. However, "the key environmental factor remains the involvement of the people who have the power to fund programs."[4]

The strategic planning process in an urban academic library is deliberately opened to a large number of players—in particular, players "who have the power to fund programs." Support of the institution is synonymous with support of the community. Not all activities within a community are supported by a single agency. Neither can an urban institution be supported by a single funding body. Thus, the number of constituencies as benefactors grows dramatically. Active solicitation of input from this diverse community of constituencies is essential throughout the planning process. When the strategic planning process advances to strategic thinking, these constituencies remain an important element of advice and support.

Each step of the strategic planning process involves risk taking, from the decision to invest time and resources in an unknown venture, through the processes of examining one's self and one's environment, to the acceptance of the necessary changes. However, the addition of representatives from a diverse group of constituencies adds additional complexity, the necessity for more cooperation, and the probability of less control—all high risk factors.

Theoretically, strategic planning should be an open process. All the key players should have a chance to provide input, process the information collected, provide recommendations, and come to consensus on the mission statement. This is possible only when the key players share a consistent vision of the organization's values and goals. The value of external participants in the planning process resides in their expertise in cognate fields, their broad perspectives on the mission of higher education and the needs and resources of the community. A variety of participants may lack sufficient knowledge of the operations and operational goals of the organization, as well as its professional traditions, institutional history, and political setting. When the group to be served and the group providing the service represent a widely divergent frame of reference, consensus on mission becomes increasingly difficult and the control of the strategic planning team harder to wend. However, the continued involvement of the community allows the environmental scan to maintain its importance as a component of a continuous information source for strategic thinking.

CONCLUSION

Strategic planning at the Auraria Library confronted the conceptual assumptions raised above by creating a planning team which would meld the operational expertise of the library staff with the broad vision of external experts. The library identified over eighty members of the academic, business, legislative, and library communities willing to participate in eight task forces covering constituencies, user services, collection quality, automation, facilities, telecommunications, personnel and organization, and resource development. Eight internal library resource groups, mirroring the eight task forces, developed a series of charges and questions to initiate the work of the task forces. The goals of the strategic planning process were to create a mission based upon the values audit and the environmental scan, to address the issues of the eight task forces, and to foster strategic thinking in the library's ongoing planning process. Because the urban environment so directly relates to the urban institution and its library, the interaction between internal expertise and external vision became the crucial component of the mechanism in the strategic planning process.

ENDNOTES

1. Jerome Krase, "Urbanism and the University," *Urban Academic Librarian* 6, no. 2/7, no. 1 (Fall 1988/Spring 1989):11. This entire issue of *Urban Academic Librarian* is devoted to defining the essence of urban academic librarianship.

2. Barbara Dunlap, "The Essence of Urban Academic Librarianship," *Urban Academic Librarian* 6, no. 2/7, no. 2 (Fall 1988/Spring 1989):29.

3. R.B. Heydinger, "Using External Information in Planning: Some Tools for Expanding Our Vision and Enhancing Our Strategic Thinking." Paper presented at the Conference on Academic Renewal, Center for the Study of Higher Education, University of Michigan, Ann Arbor, June 1983. (Referenced by Robert G. Cope, "Information System Requirements for Strategic Choices," in *Environmental Scanning for Strategic Leadership*. San Francisco: Jossey-Bass, 1986.)

4. Jay J. Chung et al. "Reaction and Discussion" of M.E.L. Jacob and D.L. Rings. "Management and Strategic Planning in Urban Libraries," in *Trends in Urban Library Management: Proceedings of the Urban Library Management Institute held in October 1988 at the University of Wisconsin-Milwaukee*. Edited by Mohammed M. Aman and Donald J. Sager, p. 44. Metuchen, N.J.:Scarecrow Press, 1989.

University Libraries
and Academic Strategic Planning
at the University of Cincinnati

Linda J. Cain
William F. Louden

SUMMARY. As part of a broadly defined academic strategic planning initiative at the University of Cincinnati, the Libraries developed a five-year plan. This article describes the process including its successes and failures, documents the most positive outcomes resulting from the process, and raises several issues related to university-wide planning processes.

Strategic planning at any large, complex university seldom resembles a textbook case in planning process. The timing is never quite ideal. Too many other initiatives are underway. Administrators, faculty and staff are invariably at different levels of understanding of and commitment to the process and the goals. And it just takes too much time. These issues and others are reflected in the microcosm of University Libraries strategic planning undertaken within the broader context of academic strategic planning at the University of Cincinnati. This article describes the institutional context, the library planning process, the initial benefits of the process, and some of the problems encountered. It is a description of work in progress, which according to the textbooks, is the very nature of strategic planning.

Linda J. Cain is Dean and University Librarian at the University of Cincinnati, Cincinnati, OH. William F. Louden is Assistant University Librarian for Planning and Budget at the University of Cincinnati, Cincinnati, OH.

STRATEGIC PLANNING CONTEXT

The University of Cincinnati is a major teaching and research institution with an enrollment which exceeds 35,000 students. Academic programs range from associate and technical degrees to M.D. and Ph.D. degrees. Many of the colleges in the University originated as independent entities resulting in a highly decentralized organizational culture. Within this culture, the colleges maintain a high degree of autonomy in academic planning. The University Libraries system, which supports programs in all of the colleges, is comprised of a main social sciences and humanities library, eleven special collection, college and departmental libraries, and a media center. The Libraries employ approximately 170 FTE staff, 34 of whom hold librarian appointments, and over 200 student assistants. Librarians are part of the faculty bargaining unit, represented by the AAUP. During the strategic planning process described in this article, contract negotiations were underway between the University and the AAUP, and also between the University and District 925 of the Service Employees International Union. The latter had been recently chosen to represent university clerical workers including most of the Libraries' support staff. Members of the Libraries staff and administration participated in both negotiations.

The initiative for strategic planning originated with the Senior Vice President and Provost to whom the Dean and University Librarian reports. University-wide planning began in September of 1986 with the development of a mission statement and planning assumptions. Both documents went through several iterations and reviews by the deans and academic administrators. Upon completion of these documents, the provost charged the deans and directors to develop draft strategic plans for their units. The draft plans would be reviewed in the Provost's Office and by the Council of Deans, and they would form the basis of an academic plan for the main campus. A strategic planning process had already been completed for the medical campus.

The planning process was to take place during the 1988-89 academic year. Deans were asked to submit interim reports of progress during that year with a draft plan submitted to the Provost in June. The timetable was later revised to extend the deadline to September. A general guideline for the final plan, more relevant to colleges than to libraries, was distributed; however, the Provost did not require a standard format. It was the provost's belief that the planning process itself was as important, if not more important, than the resulting document.

Although a strategic plan was certainly needed for University Libraries, the timing of the planning process proved problematic. A key administrative position had become vacant in the summer of 1988. Although this vacancy afforded the opportunity to review and realign administrative responsibilities, it also necessitated an interim arrangement. The Dean wanted to have a new administrative organization in place before beginning the planning process. More significantly, a consultant's report on administrative staffing, made public in August 1988, recommended eliminating over 300 positions across the University, over 30 of which were in University Libraries. A response to the report was due in November, with final decisions regarding staffing reductions to be made soon thereafter. Engaging staff in a strategic planning process while jobs were in jeopardy was determined to be counterproductive. Moreover, the administrative time and energy needed to develop a response to the consultant's staffing recommendations would be considerable. Given these circumstances, library planning was delayed until January 1989. However, since the provostal clock continued to run the Libraries had a very short time frame in which to develop its strategic plan. In January, when University Libraries began the planning process, a new organizational structure had been implemented and staff reductions had been held to seven positions of which all but one were vacant. Nonetheless, there was uncertainty among the staff about the new organization, concern about the possibility of additional budget reductions, and skepticism about the positive results of any planning process.

PLANNING TO PLAN

In the initial phase of planning the Libraries' Administrative Council (i.e., the Dean and Assistant and Associate University Librarians) met to reach consensus on the purpose and anticipated result of the planning process, the organization and philosophy of the process, and a tentative timetable. Involvement of the Administrative Council at this preliminary stage was important to defining the scope and bases of the undertaking, creating a positive atmosphere out of which the planning process could proceed, establishing a strong commitment to the initiative on the part of individuals who would assume key leadership roles throughout the process, and guaranteeing a timely conclusion of the initial planning phase.

Since previous planning experience within the library system had been confined to more traditional long-range and short-term planning models, the Council invested some time in acquiring a better understanding of the concept and elements of strategic planning. Council members read recent literature on the topic and attended a presentation on strategic planning in which the similarities and differences between strategic planning and other forms of planning were delineated. This orientation to the concept and process of strategic planning was followed by consideration of issues germane to the introduction and practical application of strategic planning within the context of University Libraries.

The Council viewed the provost's planning initiative and strategic planning for libraries as offering numerous benefits. Important among these benefits were the creation of formal documents in which the University's academic units set forth their planning priorities, and the distribution and discussion of University Libraries' strategic plan among senior university administrators and academic colleagues. The contrasting of the planning priorities of academic units with those of the Libraries would provide a context for the further refinement of University Libraries' own plan as well as affording another opportunity for participation in the University's elusive academic planning process.

In even more practical terms, the Council viewed the adoption of the strategic planning model as providing a framework in which operational planning could be developed and focused along consistent lines. Future fiscal planning and management could be directed by established planning priorities. And finally, the planning model afforded a mechanism through which the library system could assess its success in achieving its priorities and adjust those priorities according to changing internal and external conditions. The Council determined that strategic planning was a viable tool which should be adopted for future library planning regardless of the University's subsequent adherence to it.

The Council agreed that the planning process must be highly participatory providing each staff member opportunities to contribute to and review the evolving plan. This open process was considered imperative in order to assure the development of a comprehensive document and to engender a sense of ownership across the library system. Further, the plan would be informed by a blending of administrative priorities and unit level concerns. Such an approach was intended to result in a focused plan and one which had inherent viability for application to future unit operational planning.

These philosophical decisions guided the development of an organizational structure for the planning process. A strategic planning committee was organized, the nucleus of which was the newly formed management group comprised of senior library administrators and middle managers. The committee was rounded out with three appointed and four elected representatives of the professional and support staff. The goal was to create a representative cadre of respected library personnel which crossed functional and classification lines and which would provide the expertise necessary to develop a workable strategic plan. The charge to the committee was to provide leadership, to collect and synthesize data, to contribute to and critique the various elements of the plan, and to communicate the planning process and its purpose to the staff.

Within this organizational structure, the role of the Dean was viewed as crucial to the success of the entire endeavor. Without the clear commitment of the Dean, the process and its anticipated result could be jeopardized. Thus, it was agreed that the Dean would lead the library system through the planning process in the highly visible role as chair of the strategic planning committee.

Beyond library personnel appointed to the strategic planning committee, two additional groups had important roles in the process. The staff at large would participate throughout the planning process by reacting to draft documents developed by the committee. Each member of the staff would be assured opportunities to refine and focus succeeding versions of the strategic plan. This approach guaranteed both grassroot involvement and strategically timed forums for formal communication and discussion. A second group, the university library committee, would serve as a review board following the creation of the draft plan, but prior to its formal adoption. Although appropriate, the role of the library committee was somewhat dictated by the provost's final time schedule which resulted in much of the draft review process occurring during the summer months when many committee members were not available.

GETTING STARTED — A PLANNING RETREAT

Strategic planning committee members were provided with articles and citations on the concept and practice of strategic planning, and a tentative timeline was established. Soon thereafter, the committee gathered to participate in the three day retreat which focused on the task at hand. The setting chosen for the retreat was a small seminary located several miles from the university campus in another part of the city. While participants returned to their homes following each day's activities, the organization of the retreat as well as its setting encouraged committee members to become absorbed in the strategic planning process through isolating them from their day to day work responsibilities.

The retreat was conducted by a staff member from ARL's Office of Management Services. Activities adhered to a predetermined agenda which led participants progressively through the fundamental elements and techniques of strategic planning. Although modified to correspond to the local environment, the agenda replicated similar planning retreats conducted by ARL for the library systems at M.I.T., the University of Chicago, and SUNY-Buffalo. The facilitator focused the process, and elicited and coalesced the ideas and decisions reached by the group. A variety of learning techniques were employed including both lecture and nominal group activities.

The retreat agenda was divided into three basic components. The first afforded participants with an orientation to strategic planning in conceptual terms with ample opportunity for clarification of concepts and terminology. The second component focused on a practical application of strategic planning in the context of University Libraries' own planning initiative. Seventy-five percent of the retreat was allocated to this component. Utilizing the learning techniques noted above, committee members reached consensus decisions on the major elements of the planning model. These elements were a vision statement, an assessment and evaluation document, and a delineation of major programmatic areas.

To develop what would later become the asessment and evaluation document, major events in the university's history which were considered influential in the evolution of University Libraries were noted. Then the current environment in which the Libraries must carry out its responsibilities was discussed. The outcomes of these two activities were combined with the results of a frank discussion of University Libraries' strengths and weaknesses. This activity was followed by an initial attempt to develop a vision statement for the library system. This task proved to be exceptionally difficult. Four scenarios developed at ARL were used to focus thinking about the library of the future. While several important concepts would be identified in the draft vision statement, the group was not satisfied with the document as a whole. Participants then identified major programmatic or "key result" areas in which improvements were required and in which success was essential to reaching University Libraries' vision of itself in the future. The list of key result areas was narrowed to five broad categories (i.e., resources; services; personnel; technology; facilities) in which action would result in the greatest benefit. For each of these five key result areas, subgroups were formed and charged with developing a list of goals which must be pursued in order to achieve the desired result in a particular area. Subgroups reported back to the full group affording an opportunity for critical review and refinement. In combination, this series of interrelated activities would form the basic conceptual structure upon which the final plan was developed.

Finally, members of the committee discussed the application of strategic planning as they understood it in the forthcoming planning initiative. The most valuable result of this third component was the identification of important issues which needed to be addressed in order to facilitate the process. Most important among these were communication mechanisms, staff involvement, and anticipated apathy and skepticism among segments of the staff.

Committee members were universally pleased with the retreat.

The outcomes proved to be highly valuable during the subsequent planning process. Without question, most successful was the development of a preliminary body of information which would later be affirmed and refined by the staff at large. Second in importance was the evolution of the committee into a team of individuals who shared a common goal and who were committed to it. Although some uncertainty continued among members of the committee, each worked effectively toward the final goal.

DEVELOPING THE PLAN

In preparation for initiating the planning process and engaging the staff at large, the Dean convened the strategic planning committee soon after the retreat to discuss again the process and the retreat, to confirm decisions reached during the retreat, and to finalize decisions on procedural issues. This preparatory meeting resulted in several crucial outcomes which proved to be determining factors throughout the forthcoming months of planning.

The committee affirmed the soundness and accuracy of its assessment of University Libraries and the programmatic areas which should be the focus of the strategic plan. Equally important, the group reached consensus on procedural matters which would direct the planning process itself. Important elements included the role of the strategic planning committee as a representative body which had responsibility for fashioning the plan, the role of the staff at large and of special committees within the organization as review groups to critique the work of the committee, and the creation of a formal and informal communication structure to be utilized with the staff in order to maintain an open and fully participatory process.

The Libraries staff at large was brought into the planning process more directly at this point. Over a five day period, departmental meetings were scheduled with subgroups of the strategic planning committee. Committee members followed an outline as they oriented staff members to the concept and practice of strategic planning, the reasons for this campus-wide initiative, the internal process which University Libraries would use to implement the planning model, and the programmatic framework developed during the retreat. The principle focus of each of the meetings was a review and discussion of the key result areas identified during the retreat. Discussion also addressed the role of the staff and the strategic planning committee throughout the process. And lastly, the meetings were intended to stress the importance of the planning initiative to the staff.

The result of these sessions was mixed at best. The committee did receive valuable ideas from staff members which contributed to further refinement of the key result areas and the development of goals or target areas for each one. Likewise, the staff at large came to better understand the internal process ahead, including their role. In general though, the level of participation by staff during these meetings was most disappointing. Moreover, a mixture of apathy and skepticism was exhibited which served to reemphasize the importance of encouraging staff involvement as the planning process proceeded.

At the conclusion of these meetings, the strategic planning committee began the task of drafting materials which reflected outcomes of the retreat and the sessions with staff. Seven subgroups were formed to prepare preliminary documents which would subsequently be presented to and reviewed by the staff. There was a group to redraft the vision statement, one to draft an assessment and evaluation document to provide a historical and environmental context for University Libraries' plan, and one group for each of the five key result areas. Each group was responsible for collecting further data as appropriate, analyzing the data, and preparing an expanded draft document to include goals and possible strategies to achieve each goal. Groups distributed their drafts to the committee as a whole and invited review and comment. Most critical during this process was the further development of goals which added substance to each of the five key result areas.

After the committee reviewed the first draft of University Libraries strategic plan, a series of meetings was scheduled for staff review and discussion. Attendance was not organized along department lines nor was participation mandatory. In advance of these review sessions, the draft plan was widely circulated among the staff. The review sessions would be the final opportunity for staff to influence the direction of the plan before the final drafting. The focus of each meeting was upon the goals and strategies outlined for each of the five programmatic or key result areas. Staff comments were recorded at each session and written comments from individual staff members were sent to the Dean. Considered as a whole, these review sessions were valuable to the further refinement of the plan although staff contribution at most sessions was modest at best. Following the staff review sessions, the strategic planning committee was convened by the Dean to discuss the merit of specific staff contributions and to decide whether or not to incorporate them. Additional recommendations also came forward from committee members.

A redrafting subcommittee composed of five committee members including the Dean was formed to distill ideas, provide clarity and continuity to the text, and reduce the broad scope of the draft. The subcommittee met intensively over a five day period. The work proved to be both difficult and tedious. From time to time, other committee members were requested to join the subcommittee in order to provide clarification and review major decisions. The outcome of this activity reshaped the draft plan in significant ways. Most significant among the changes were constricting the context of the plan to a five year period, and the development of a new key result area, Fiscal Resources. This new section was introduced in order to bring together fiscal related goals which appeared throughout the plan as well as to emphasize the importance of enhanced fiscal resources to University Libraries' achievement of its programmatic goals.

This major revision of the draft plan was distributed to members of the strategic planning committee for review and comment. Subsequently, the draft was distributed to the staff with review sessions scheduled for the following week. Three sessions were open to any library staff member, one session was designated for librarians, and one for department heads. In addition, the Dean conducted review sessions with two standing advisory groups representing the support staff and the librarians. The final revision of the plan was endorsed by the staff with mostly modest but some substantive changes suggested. This review also served as a basis for communication of University Libraries' planning priorities which were intended to guide system-wide and unit level decisions well into the next decade. After final editing the draft of the strategic plan was submitted to the provost and distributed to the staff in mid-September.

The document set forth planning priorities for the forthcoming five years (1990-1995), and it included twenty-six goals in five key result areas (i.e., Resources and Services; Human Resources; Technology; Facilities; and Fiscal Resources). At least two but never more than eight strategies were associated with each goal. An overview, vision statement, and a history of University Libraries with assessment of internal and external environments and strengths and weaknesses were included in the document.

PRESENTATION AND REVIEW

During the Fall and early Winter of the 1989-90 academic year University Libraries' strategic plan underwent wider review. The plan was presented to and reviewed by the University Library Committee with discussion of the plan providing an excellent introduction to library issues for new members of this group. In addition, it provided a context in which to address some specific concerns of committee members. Also during the Fall and early Winter each dean and director presented a summary of individual college strategic plans at a series of meetings with the deans and appropriate administrative staff. These presentations provided an opportunity for all the deans to gain a better understanding of the planning priorities of other colleges and units, and to identify common themes among the plans. The presentations were especially valuable for the Dean and University Librarian who has responsibility for providing library support for instructional and research programs across the campus. This forum also provided an opportunity to educate university administrators and other deans about academic library issues in general and University Libraries' programs in particular. Rather than presenting a comprehensive overview of the entire plan, the Dean and University Librarian chose to emphasize elements of the plan which would require cooperative action between the Libraries and the college deans and faculties. The evolving world of scholarly information, the changing balance between collections and "access," and the problems of preserving collections were also major themes.

In the best of all possible worlds, one might have expected that appropriate librarians would have been involved in the strategic planning of the colleges and that, at the very least, recognition of library support for expanding or new academic programs would be cited in college strategies. In reality, only three college plans out of a total of thirteen made any reference at all to library resources — some without consultation with the appropriate librarian, and others with only cursory consultation. Only one college included a librarian on its strategic planning committee. On the positive side, the process which mandated review and discussion by the Council of Deans before finalizing the plans provided librarians with the opportunity to react to college plans and to recommend strategies to address issues of library support.

At the time of this writing, strategic plans are still under review in the Provost's Office with the intent to develop a draft academic plan for review and approval by the Deans. Future budget requests from the colleges and libraries will be evaluated in light of the approved academic plan and the strategic plans from each unit.

REFLECTIONS

The outcome of the strategic planning process at the University level remains to be seen. For University Libraries, however, the process has proved very valuable. The plan has provided a framework for operational goals and decisions. The planning process focused staff attention on library-wide issues and programs, and it provided a context for departmental responsibilities and individual jobs. The entire staff was given the opportunity to consider University Libraries as a whole — where we've been, what we do well, what we need to improve — and to contribute to setting directions for the future. Although a small percentage of the staff took the opportunity to contribute, those contributions were thoughtful and valuable. As an organization, we reaffirmed our commitment to service and to staff training and development. We outlined for ourselves, and for the campus community, the rapid changes taking place in libraries and in the world of information delivery.

The process has also been valuable relative to the Libraries' relationship with other university units. One of the emphases in the Libraries' plan was greater involvement in academic planning across the campus. Immediately following the Libraries' presentation to the Deans, three proposals for new degree programs were forwarded to the Dean for review. Based upon academic priorities stated in college plans, library administrators and bibliographers can initiate discussions with the colleges concerning library support for planned program changes and enhancements.

What would we change if we had it to do over again? We would plan the process over an eighteen month rather than a nine month period, and we would invest more time on the assessment of the environment and on an evaluation of the Libraries' strengths and weaknesses. Timing the process is critical both in relation to the total length of time allotted and in relation to other activities being undertaken at the same time. Ideally, strategic planning should not be undertaken during prolonged labor/management negotiations. The energies of members of the strategic planning committee were often diverted from the planning initiative toward this and a myriad of other library-related issues. Draft planning documents should have undergone far more revision before we asked for staff review. In retrospect, we gave staff too much paper to read and critique in too short a time. The most cogent critiques occurred with the final draft which was substantially condensed and consistently formatted.

What about the University strategic planning process? Campus-wide academic planning began in 1986. By mid-1990, the process is still underway. The process has been successful in providing a forum for discussing university-wide issues in a very decentralized environment. Issues such as retention of students, ethnic and cultural diversity, and faculty and staff development have been addressed by each college in substantive ways through their strategic plans. Academic planning with a unified view of future academic emphases has been more elusive; however, that is to be expected in any multiversity. Whatever the nature of the final academic plan, it has clearly taken too long to develop. A university engaging in a planning process of this magnitude must allocate staff with appropriate skills, support and time to the endeavor. This was not consistently the case at the University of Cincinnati due to staff changes and conflicting commitments. Finally, there must be a common understanding of which elements of planning will be "top down" and which will be "bottom up" — always a difficult issue on a university campus.

A Strategic Planning Process
for the Multi-Campus University System:
The Role of One Campus and Its Library

Leslie A. Manning

SUMMARY. The purpose of this paper is to present an overview of the strategic planning process as it was adapted by the multi-campus system of the University of Colorado with a close look at its application at the University of Colorado at Colorado Springs campus and the campus library. This overview will provide a picture of the application of planning techniques through the various administrative tiers of the university. And will place library strategic planning in its proper perspective: planning for a subunit of a multi-part organization responding to an external environment.

Alice:	"Would you tell me, please, which way I ought to go from here?"
Cheshire Cat:	"That depends . . . on where you want to get to."
Alice:	"I don't much care where—"
Cheshire Cat:	"Then it doesn't matter which way you go."

Alice's Adventures in Wonderland,—Lewis Carroll

INTRODUCTION

The often quoted and paraphrased exchange between Alice and the Cat clearly illustrates the principles of strategic planning. Strategic planning, a common practice of successful military powers for centuries, was first described for the business community in the

---

Leslie A. Manning is Dean of Libraries at the University of Colorado, Colorado Springs, CO.

sixties by Alfred Chandler, Jr. in his book, *Strategy and Structure: Chapters in the History of the Industrial Enterprise*. However, it wasn't until the appearance of George Keller's book, *Academic Strategy*, in 1983 that strategic planning techniques began replacing earlier planning methods in the administrative offices of college and university campuses.

The strategic planning concepts presented by Keller have been well received in academic circles, in large part, due to the climate of the eighties. Colleges and universities are entering a period of extraordinary change accompanied with pervasive problems.

This revolutionary era includes more than just the declining enrollments of traditionally aged college students. Other demographic issues such as the increasing numbers of minority and foreign students, returning older students, and aging faculty are set against a backdrop of technological changes, deteriorating scientific equipment, and deteriorating facilities. Student emphasis is career-oriented. There is increasing competition among institutions of higher education and those with corporate training programs. It is also a time of uncertain and declining federal and state support accompanied by increasing federal and state controls and demands. With so much turbulence internally and externally, it is little wonder that a planning method that seeks to merge the two and give new direction to institutions has been so widely embraced.[1]

DEFINITIONS

What is strategic planning? The general dictionary definitions of strategy refer to its use in the military setting as the art of directing and projecting by the commander-in-chief. It is a plan for successful action based on the rationality and interdependence of the moves of the opposition. The definitions distinguish strategy from tactics. Tactics is defined as the mechanical movement of bodies set in motion by strategies; the localized hostilities or battles where adversaries are in contact. Strategy is planning where and how to fight while tactics is fighting the battles.

Alfred Chandler defined strategic planning in business as "the determination of basic long-term goals and objectives of an enterprise, and the adoption of courses of action and the allocation of resources necessary for carrying out these goals."[2]

This has been refered to as the "ends-ways-means" model of strategic planning where "ends" are goals and objectives, "ways" are courses of action to realize goals and objectives, and "means" are resources necessary for carrying out these goals. Peter Drucker defines strategic planning as "the continuous process of making present entrepreneurial (*risk-taking*) *decisions* systematically and with the greatest knowledge of their futurity; organizing the *efforts* needed to carry out these decisions; and measuring the results of the decisions against the expectations through organized, *systematic feedback*."[3]

Strategic planning helps a business answer three questions. The answer to the first, "Where are you going?" provides the business with a vision. The second, "What is the environment?" requires an examination of the internal and external environment to identify opportunities, threats, alternatives and gaps. And, the third, "How do you get there?" brings the business to the point of identifying strategies, developing contingency and operations plans with an evaluation mechanism.[4]

A frequently used metaphor for comparing strategic planning to earlier methods of planning is that of comparing the use of the compass to the road map. The compass identifies the general direction of travel while the road map identifies the specific path and turns to take.

The business community has continually refined strategic planning techniques over the past twenty five years. One refinement identified by Robert H. Hayes in the early eighties was the need to place greater emphasis on the qualitative rather than the quantitative. He cautioned managers to keep strategic planning from becoming a set of detailed plans developed by "counters" rather than "doers." Strategic planning must be done in a participatory manner from the lowest levels of the organization. It is not forecasting but rather the identification of a general direction and vision. It also needs to be the development and building of staff capabilities and resources within the organization rather than a sole reliance on financial resources to accomplish goals. If U.S. businesses are to remain competitive in the world economy, these changes from earlier strategic planning techniques are essential.[5]

The use of strategic planning in higher education occurred after the business community had the opportunity to identify and correct weaknesses in strategic planning techniques. Like the Japanese who entered the electronic age late, the academy will be using tried, tested and improved methods of strategic planning. This advantage may lead higher education through these turbulent times into a period of greater achievement and vitality.[6]

STRATEGIC PLANNING MODELS FOR COLLEGES AND UNIVERSITIES

Keller, like so many authors on strategic planning, first defines strategic planning by exclusion and then describes its six major elements. In summary, Keller views strategic planning as an active decision-making process to identify and shape the destiny of the institution in light of the institution's current character and its future identity in a changing competitive environment. It is a participatory process that is highly tolerant of controversy; focuses on the fate of the institution as a whole; and is continuous, pervasive and indigenous within the culture of the institution.[7] Robert Cope provides a more recent definition informed by several years of the use of strategic planning in colleges and universities.

> Strategic planning is an open systems approach to steering an enterprise over time through uncertain environmental waters. It is a proactive, problem-solving behavior directed externally at conditions in the environment and a means to find a favorable competitive position in the continual competition for resources. Its primary purpose is to achieve success with mission while linking the institution's future to anticipated changes in the environment in such a way that the acquisition of resources (money, personnel, students, good will) is faster than the depletion of resources.[8]

Cope further emphasizes that strategic planning has the essential characteristics of relating the *whole* institution to the *whole* environment. Cope's definition differs from Keller's in its stress on the institution's resources and on implementation of the strategy. Implementation of the strategy is the shaping of the enterprise which includes allocation of resources; arrangement of structure and organization; and development of staff, faculty and students within the campus culture.[9]

In higher education as within business, the key ingredients to successful strategic planning are leadership, information and people.[10] Leadership is an intangible concept that is difficult to define. In the strategic planning process, it is that quality of an individual to touch people's nerve endings and cause them to act; to keep the mere routine from becoming acceptable. Vision doesn't necessarily have to come from the leader but he must meld it from the views obtained in a participatory culture. The leader inspires the organization to act upon the vision. Leadership is essential to integrate the visioning with the implementation of strategy.[11]

The awareness of the importance of the external environment on planning is the single most important contribution of strategic planning to higher education. Keller estimated that for most colleges and universities over 75% of all changes were triggered by outside factors such as state and federal actions.[12] Thus information about the external environment is a key ingredient to strategic planning. The gathering and reporting of this external environmental information is refered to as "environmental scanning" or futures research techniques. Data in the area of demographics, economics, technology and socio-political data are important elements of the environment scan.

Internal information about the institution is also critical. The internal information needed is more than that currently gathered by most universities' management information systems. Information about internal operations, curricular and program data, faculty and student information, and student outcomes data, are all needed. Also needed is "intelligence" information which comes from informal networks and may not be quantifiable. Current, accurate but not necessarily extensive or detailed information is essential to rational decision-making and the strategic planning process.[13]

People are the third ingredient for a successful strategic planning process. It is critical that it be people, specially selected and trained, acting in a participatory fashion with lofty aims and exercising quality controls. A consultative style with an emphasis on team building will encourage participation. The strength of the process will come with a "bottom-up" approach. This collegiality has historically been a strength in most American colleges and universities.[14] The consultative process is also the key element many have attributed to the Japanese business superiority over American businesses.

CONTEXT – THE UNIVERSITY OF COLORADO

The University of Colorado is a four campus system. Each campus has a unique function within Colorado higher education. The 600 acre main campus, founded in 1876 at Boulder, is a traditional state university with a broad range of undergraduate and graduate programs and professional programs. The 420 acre Colorado Springs campus, founded in 1966, provides a selective number of programs at the undergraduate and graduate level in general education and professional disciplines. The University of Colorado at Denver is located in the heart of downtown Denver on the Auraria campus, a physical facility shared with the Community College of Denver and Metropolitan State College. UC Denver serves the urban population with a range of general education and professional programs at the graduate and undergraduate level. The 40 acre campus of the University Health Sciences Center is also located in Denver. It provides programs in nursing, dentistry, medicine, and pharmacy and includes the University Hospital, Colorado Psychiatric Hospital and eight research institutes.

The University of Colorado is governed by a nine member Board of Regents elected on a state-wide and regional basis. The Regents are charged with the general supervision of the University including all its funds. A President, appointed by the Regents, serves as the chief academic officer of the system. He delegates the responsibility of running each campus to a Chancellor. Faculty participate in campus governance through a Faculty Senate and in system governance through a system-wide Faculty Council. Staff also participate in governance at the campus and system levels. The Board of Regents reports to the Colorado Legislature through the Colorado Commission on Higher Education (CCHE). The CCHE was reconstituted in 1984 with the authority to distribute state funding, establish role and mission, approve new programs, delete redundant programs, accept master plans, approve capital construction, approve tuition increases, etc.

In 1985, the Board of Regents appointed a dynamic and energetic new president to the University of Colorado. During his first year he identified a number of issues. Foremost among these was poor external relations with CU constituents; the citizens of Colorado, the state legislature and other state institutions of higher education. Human resource issues were also paramount in the areas of faculty expectations, diversity, and the state personnel system for classified employees. Further, there was no clear understanding across the system as to the mission of either central administration or any one of the campuses.

In addition to these unique issues, the University faced the same growing concerns of other colleges and universities. The decreasing number of high school graduates, increasing need for minority educational opportunity, and increasing external controls from the federal and state governments. In Colorado like other states, there was a growing tendency to fund specific projects or programs rather than provide across the board increases at the necessary levels.

Thus, in conjunction with discussions with the Board of Regents and his administrative team, the President decided in 1986 to initiate a strategic planning process to be coordinated through the office of the newly appointed Vice President for Academic Affairs. This was excellent timing as there were new chief officers on all four campuses as well as at the central offices.

Strategic Planning Structure — System-Wide

A key element of the strategic planning structure was the total involvement of top administrators in the central systems office. The President and the Vice President for Academic Affairs spear-headed the process with assistance from the Director of the Office of Policy and Planning. The Vice President for Human Resources, Assistant Vice President for Research, and the Vice President for Budget and Finance were all key participants. The Board of Regents encouraged, supported and discussed on an ongoing basis the progress and direction of the process.

The Chancellors, Vice Chancellors for Academic Affairs, Budget Officers and Planning Officers of each campus were also involved in the system-wide process. These two groups comprised a system-wide planning council that closely monitored progress and shared information.

The President initiated the process with a letter to all university employees enclosed in their August 1986 paycheck envelope. His letter called for participation of all in identifying the university's future and a commitment from all to achieve that future. He also informed the staff that within the next month he would distribute a paper describing his personal vision for CU. That paper, *Toward the Twenty-first Century*, further described the need for planning; urged participation and commitment; and identified principles upon which he felt CU should move forward. The paper identified the areas of human resources; the importance of diversity; the need to provide a "civic education"; and the responsibilities of a public university to the state as the main areas of focus.

Process — System-Wide

The overall process was divided into three initial phases which were followed with ongoing evaluation and reassessment. The first phase was to conduct a situational analysis, the second was to determine strategic goals and objectives at the campus level, and the third phase was to link strategic goals and objectives to the financial planning process of the university.

The strategic planning process was initiated with the hiring of a consultant to conduct an Environmental Scan in the summer of 1986. The results of the scan were reported to the newly constituted system-wide planning council in fall of 1986 at a one day retreat held on the Boulder campus. In addition to the scan, documents on human resources, graduate education, undergraduate education, economic development, and space sciences were discussed. The group was then given a planning calendar to be followed by each campus in the development of a campus strategic plan. A completed statement from each campus was presented to the Regents in the spring of 1987 and distributed in booklet form to the campus communities in fall 1987.

The final request budget for the 1987-88 year was prepared and presented to the Regents based, as much as the late date would allow, on the strategic plan of each campus. The initial and final budget requests for each subsequent year have been based on the campus' strategic plan. Achievements of the campus-level strategic plan are reported annually to the Regents in a half-day meeting held each spring.

Each campus has a unique process for developing, updating and implementing its strategic plan. The President's *Toward the Twenty-first Century*, the other documents prepared at the central offices, and the environmental scan were used as a basis from which each campus identified and developed its initial vision or mission statement, goals, and strategies to achieve the goals. Program reviews, accreditation reviews, and the state mandated five year master planning process have also influenced the evolution of the strategic plan.

Several common issues appeared in the statements of each campus. These were then identified as cross cutting-issues that needed to be addressed at the system level. Follow up committees were appointed to address these issues. Each year new issues are identified and analyzed.

The President continues to inform staff of the progress of strategic planning through the monthly letters in their paychecks. He also distributed two follow up booklets on the progress of the strategic planning process. The booklets were also widely distributed to the external community and the state legislature.

Outcomes — System-Wide

The major outcomes of the strategic plan at the system level include:

1. development of strategic plans for the four campuses;
2. development of a process wherein academic planning drives the budget;
3. improvement of external relations with the citizens of Colorado, industry and business, the state legislature, and other state academic institutions;
4. encouragement of a higher quality educational experience at the undergraduate level;

5. increased fund raising efforts;
6. support for human resource initiatives and diversity: and
7. effective progress in the legislative arena with the Hospital legislation.

The system-wide process gave a high priority to image building in order to engender a sense of ownership among constituents around the state. The rewards have been significant. The new image has helped attract new resources to the University Foundation; created a greater sense of community within the University; helped secure increases in state funding for higher education; and insured success with two key legislative issues.

To date, the strategic planning process has been campus driven. The advantage of this approach has been to return a sense of responsibility and authority to each campus. However, it is now time for a more definitive strategic plan at the system level, explaining the role of the system vis-à-vis the campuses. This is evident in the difficulty surrounding the cross-cutting issues. These issues have become competitive with specific strategic issues on campuses. Further there are issues which can only be addressed at the system level such as how the system might assist the newer, smaller campuses to develop; what resources should be centralized and shared by the four campuses; etc.

The process began with the development of statements in the 1986-87 academic year and has been followed by three years of implementation. The environment, especially the economic and political ones have changed dramatically. It would be wise to reassess the process, applaud the accomplishments, and begin afresh with updated assessments of the external and internal environments.

CONTEXT – COLORADO SPRINGS CAMPUS

The University of Colorado at Colorado Springs (UCCS) is the smallest of the four campuses of the university system. It was established in 1966 as an extension campus and became an autonomous campus in 1972. It is a commuter campus located on 68 of its 420 acres. It has realized increasing enrollments in all of its years except one in the early eighties. But, by 1986 that growth had slowed to 2% each year. In 1989-90 with an annual operating budget of $20 million, there are 4,000 student FTE with a head count of approximately 6,000 students. The faculty consists of 225 FTE and the staff number 187 FTE.

The campus offers a selective number of degree programs in the five colleges of Education: Letters, Arts and Sciences; Business; Engineering; and Public Administration. The professional schools offer masters degrees and a PhD in Electrical Engineering. The College of Letters, Arts and Science offers only seventeen undergraduate degree options and six masters degrees. In 1986, the Colorado Commission on Higher Education (CCHE) authorized the offering of coordinated degrees within the system. This allows UCCS to offer degrees through coordination with the Boulder and Denver campuses.

The 1983 statutory statement defining UCCS' role and mission refers to it as a comprehensive baccalaureate liberal arts and science institution with selected professional programs and such graduate programs as will serve the needs of the Colorado Springs region. It also states that UCCS will have selective admission standards instead of the highly selective admission standards of the other three campuses. The role and mission statement and admission standards are amended through the five-year master planning process of the CCHE.

In 1986 the President appointed a farsighted and seasoned administrator from the Boulder and Denver campuses to serve as the Chancellor of the UCCS campus. The Chancellor identified a number of issues. First as a result of frequent turnover in the chancellor's position, there was little or no teamwork at top administrative levels; there were conflicting views of the campus' mission; there was no coordination between existing plans such as the CCHE master plan, accreditation reports, budgets and programs reviews. Also, there had been conflicting direction from the central administration regarding mission, authority and responsibility.

The Chancellor also found numerous strengths. The small size and lack of entrenched history of the campus gives it tremendous flexibility. It has an excellent image in the local community with strong community support for the institution. The faculty and staff are sound and offer a quality undergraduate education in part due to a low student/faculty ratio. Though somewhat cyclical, Colorado Springs is a growing and developing community with emphasis on electronics, military and service industries. Further the Colorado Springs area is nationally known for its natural beauty, its pleasant year-round climate, and its attractive quality of life.

The Chancellor enthusiastically endorsed the President's desire to initiate a strategic planning process as a means of addressing some of the issues and capitalizing on the strengths.

Structure — Colorado Springs Campus

Each of the four campuses of the University of Colorado took a different approach in developing its strategic plan. The UCCS campus did not and does not have a Planning Office or position to which it could assign the major responsibility of the effort. Further, the Chancellor and the President both agreed that the process chosen required significant participation by the entire campus community. Thus, the Chancellor appointed the Library Director to serve as the campus' member of the System-wide Planning Council and co-chair of a campus taskforce of faculty and staff. The Planning Task-force was charged with developing a vision statement and identifying strategic goals and objectives with the broadest campus participation.

The Planning Taskforce was co-chaired by the Distinguished Professor of the College of Business. Faculty representatives from all colleges were appointed as were several staff and student representatives. Early in the process, the Chancellor also appointed a community advisory committee to provide additional input into the outcomes.

Process — Colorado Springs Campus

The Chancellor appointed the Planning Taskforce early in the fall semester 1986. The taskforce established a calendar of tasks in keeping with the calendar issued by the President's office. It then reviewed existing planning documents, accreditation self-studies and reports, and other pertinent documents generated on the campus. The taskforce then designed a plan to obtain campus participation.

A series of presentations were offered to the campus community to provide them with the insights the taskforce had gained from reviewing existing documents and to inform them of the results of the environmental scanning process. These informational presentations were followed in the fall of 1986 by two campus-wide brainstorming meetings moderated by two Business School faculty who specialize in group interaction, team-building and planning. These campus-wide sessions were lively and informative "pep" talks followed by extensive discussions of issues, opportunities, strengths and directions.

The goal of the first session was to instill a sense of responsibility and teamwork as well as identify issues and directions. The taskforce then synthesized the input and compiled a draft vision statement, a list of major issues, and possible directions. The goal of the second session was to respond to the taskforce's vision statement, select six to eight major issues, and identify strategic directions. The taskforce once again synthesized the input into a final draft for campus-wide review and then forwarded the document to the president's office early in the spring semester 1987.

The taskforce was then disbanded although its members have been called upon to moderate small group discussions in follow-up sessions over the past three years. Each academic year, there are two to four campus-wide strategic planning meetings to review and revise the plan as necessary. Also the sessions are used to keep the campus informed of accomplishments and shifts in direction. In the spring of 1988, Deans and Directors of campus units began making brief presentations about their unit's planning process and accomplishments in relation to the campus strategic plan.

As a result of these presentations, it became clear that there was a lack of coordination with respect to recruitment and retention activities. As a result of recommendations from the planning sessions, a Student Recruitment and Retention Council was appointed and is in the process of drafting a strategic plan to address this issue due in May 1990.

Outcomes — Colorado Springs Campus

The UCCS strategic plan emphasized five major directions with its eight goals, including:

1. Increased enrollment and income from non-state funding;
2. Improved undergraduate and graduate education;

3. Improved staff and faculty development and benefits;
4. Enhanced relations with the community and businesses; and
5. Insured diversity of students, faculty, staff and programs.

The accomplishments related to these strategies are numerous and include the following selected items:

1. Commitment by the CU System to UCCS' goal to become a comprehensive university;
2. Establishing interdisciplinary centers to provide new program focus, rather than reallocation of resources from existing programs;
3. Increasing student enrollment at a rate of 5% per year;
4. Increasing numbers of minority student enrollment;
5. Receipt of a $2.5 million grant to improve the teaching of core skills at the undergraduate level;
6. Support for the PhD in Electrical Engineering and Masters in Space Operations;
7. Increasing visibility and recognition in the community;
8. Significant communication with the City and County government, the Chamber of Commerce, and the Economic Development Council as well as with numerous businesses in the area;
9. Improving support for services such as computing, library, public relations, and foundation;
10. Completion of a master plan changing UCCS status from a commuter campus to one with dormitories; and
11. Maintaining the low student/faculty ratio.

The process has served to invigorate staff who have made significant use of innovative ideas to improve service and teamwork across the campus. It has also given the campus a sense of its future and control over its destiny. At the same time it has allowed for individual initiative. For some, however, progress has not been dramatic enough or fast enough. The process has been successful because from the start it was in the hands of the campus as a whole and not the sole purview of a planning officer.

The strategic planning process at UCCS is now at a cross-road not unlike the one faced by the system-wide process. The goals and strategies need a fresh look with clearer ties to each unit and its goals. Due to the limited funding flexibility of a small budget, greater focus on two or three main areas is needed.

CONTEXT — UCCS LIBRARY

The UCCS Library, like the campus, is only 25 years old. It serves the campus community with a staff of 22 FTE, one third of whom are student employees, one third of whom are classified staff and one third of whom are librarians. It offers the basic services of an academic library including reference, on-line searching, circulation, reserves, interlibrary loan and bibliographic instruction. It also acquires and processes a collection for access of 550,000 items, over half of which are in microforms. Its collection is limited both by its age (most items have imprints of 1975 or later), its size, and its materials budget of just over $500,000 per year. The physical facility is new and inviting, although beginning to become crowded.

Due to limitations of the collection, access and instruction have been concepts basic to the strong service ethic of the library. Due to the small size of the campus, librarians have been actively involved in all aspects of faculty governance and curriculum development. In 1985, a program review by an external evaluation team identified these and many other strengths and needs.

In 1986, the Chancellor appointed a new Library Director. She found not only the above mentioned strengths, but also a desire on the part of library staff and faculty for change and involvement in that change.

Structure — UCCS Library

The strategic planning of a campus unit was not specifically identified as part of the University of Colorado strategic planning process. However, it was evident that a more successful library strategic plan could be developed if it was done in conjunction with the system and campus process. Since the Library Director was deeply involved in the system and campus process, she spear-headed the process within the Library. All library classified staff and faculty participated through the monthly staff meeting forum. Student employees were not part of the forum except by passing ideas on to the staff. A Library Advisory Committee of faculty and students from outside the library also provided input into the process.

Process — Library

The library staff reviewed the system-wide documents and the campus vision and strategic goals and objectives. They provided the Director with input on the strategic direction and goals for the library. The Director synthesized this input into goals and objective statements. Due to the number of objectives, eight to ten were identified by the staff as priorities for each year. The resulting statement was then presented to the newly formed Library Advisory Committee in the fall semester of 1987.

Once a quarter, a discussion of accomplishments and issues occurs in the monthly staff meeting. Annually each spring the document is revised and major priorities for the upcoming year are identified. The goals and objectives are also incorporated into the individual evaluation process for both faculty and staff.

In spring 1988, the Director made a presentation to the campus-wide strategic planning meeting and to the Regents on the planning process and the UCCS Library and its relation to the campus and system strategic planning process. The budget request for each year is also tied to the library, campus and system strategic plan.

Outcomes — UCCS Library

The outcomes of the Library's strategic plan reflect the same basic strategies found above for the system and the campus. Major priorities include:

1. Enhancing service and support for undergraduate and graduate education;
2. Expanding the community and business partnership;
3. Expanding collections to meet program needs; and
4. Enhancing staff and faculty development.

As a result of these strategies the following accomplishments have been realized:

1. Installed an integrated automated system;
2. Established an archives and publications exchange program;
3. Increased the materials budget to provide for new academic programs;
4. Encouraged and supported staff development and participation within the library and throughout the campus;
5. Improved communications within the Library and outside the Library to ensure a more informed staff and community; and
6. Established a fee-based reference service for local businesses.

There are clearly many more areas needing improvement, enhancement or reorganization. The Library's strategic planning document lists numerous projects needing attention. Those receiving first attention, however, are those most closely matching the direction of the campus as a whole. The Library process will need to be reassessed to meet any changes made in the system and campus process and strategies.

The process of strategic planning was a new one to the Library and its staff. Earlier planning efforts had been incremental and were conducted in isolation of the campus and system as a whole and without an examination of the environment.

CONCLUSION

The University of Colorado multi-campus strategic planning process fits the classic definition of strategic planning found in the literature. It successfully employs the techniques of visioning by comparing university strengths to environmental opportunities, participation at the broadest possible level, and tying directions to resources. Each campus within the system has developed its unique strategic plan following these same basic principles. The results are renewed vitality, improved quality and growth. Within the context of the broader planning process, the Library has implemented a strategic planning process that insures that it moves in concert with the campus and system.

The value of strategic planning is in its requirement that planning be done on a whole institution basis with awareness of the whole surrounding environment. Academic libraries have long done their planning as autonomous units without concern for the broader context. However, it is this broader context that lends focus to planning and real direction to the library.

REFERENCES

1. George Keller, *Academic Strategy: the Management Revolution in American Higher Education* (Baltimore, Maryland: The Johns Hopkins University Press, 1983), p. 3-26.

2. Alfred D. Chandler, Jr., *Strategy and Structure: Chapters in the History of the Industrial Enterprise* (Cambridge, Mass.: The M.I.T. Press, 1962), p. 13.

3. Peter F. Drucker, *Management: Tasks, Responsibilities, Practices* (New York: Harper & Row, Publishers, 1974), p. 125.

4. Benton E. Gup, *Guide to Strategic Planning* (New York: McGraw-Hill Book Company, 1980), p. 11-23.

5. Robert H. Hayes, "Strategic Planning—Forward in Reverse?" *Harvard Business Review*, 63(November-December 1985): 118.

6. Keller, *Academic Strategy*, p. ix.

7. Ibid., p. 140-164.

8. Robert G. Cope, *Opportunity from Strength: Strategic Planning Clarified with Case Examples*, ASHE-ERIC Higher Education Report No. 8 (Washington, D.C.: Association for the Study of Higher Education, 1987), p. 3.

9. Ibid., p. 6.

10. Keller, *Academic Strategy*, p. 125-137.

11. Cope, *Opportunity from Strength*, p. 7.

12. Keller, *Academic Strategy*, p. 145.

13. Ibid., p. 131-133.

14. Ibid., p. 163.

BIBLIOGRAPHY

Aggarwal, Raj. "Systematic Strategic Planning at a State University: A Case Study of Adapting Corporate Planning Techniques." *Innovative Higher Education*. 11(Spring/Summer 1987): 123-135.

Chandler, Alfred D., Jr. *Strategy and Structure: Chapters in the History of the Industrial Enterprise*. Cambridge, Mass.: The M.I.T. Press, 1962.

Cope, Robert G. *Opportunity from Strength: Strategic Planning Clarified with Case Examples*. ASHE-ERIC Higher Education Report No. 8. Washington, D.C.: Association for the Study of Higher Education, 1987.

Drucker, Peter F. *Management: Tasks, Responsibilities, Practices*. New York: Harper & Row, Publishers, 1974.

Gee, E. Gordon. *A Statement to the University Community*. Boulder, Colo.: University of Colorado, October 1988.

Gee, E. Gordon. *A Summary of Strategic Planning at the University of Colorado: A Report to the University Community*. Boulder, Colo.: University of Colorado, April 1989.

Gee, E. Gordon. *The University of Colorado: Toward the Twenty-first Century*. Boulder, Colo.: University of Colorado, Fall 1986.

Gilley, J. Wade; Fulmer, Kenneth A. and Reithlingshoefer, Sally J. *Searching for Academic Excellence: Twenty Colleges and Universities on the Move and Their Leaders*. New York: American Council of Education, Macmillan Publishing Company, 1986.

Gup, Benton E. *Guide to Strategic Planning*. New York: McGraw-Hill Book Company, 1980.

Hayes, Robert H. "Strategic planning – forward in reverse?" *Harvard Business Review*. 63(November-December 1985): 111-119.

Keller, George. *Academic Strategy: the Management Revolution in American Higher Education*. Baltimore, Maryland: The Johns Hopkins University Press, 1983.

Shirley, Robert C. "Identifying the Levels of Strategy for a College or University." *Long Range Planning*. 16(June 1983): 92-99.

Toward the Twenty-first Century . . . . : Strategic Planning at the University of Colorado. Boulder, Colo.: University of Colorado, Summer 1987.

A Strategic Planning Imperative:
The Penn State Experience

Nancy M. Cline
Salvatore M. Meringolo

SUMMARY. Strategic planning is best operationalized as part of a broader set of strategic management principles in which it is viewed as a platform for improving organizational communication and development, resource allocation, and the overall management framework. There are no singular, prescriptive approaches to strategic planning. The emphasis should be placed on strategic thinking and acting, rather than on process. The Pennslyvania State University has adopted a comprehensive planning process that is uncommon because it links the multi-year strategic plans of its various units to the annual budget cycle. The strategic plan thus provides a blueprint for the operation of the University Libraries.

"Some act and think later — and they think more of excuses than consequences. Others think neither before nor after. The whole of life should be spent thinking about how to find the right course of action to follow." (attributed to Spanish Jesuit Baltasar Gracian three and one-half centuries ago)[1]

Strategic planning can be an integral tool in the management of the contemporary organization. It has been widely applied in such not-for-profit organizations as federal and state agencies, urban organizations such as fire and police departments, as well as in hospitals and health care organizations, colleges and universities, and libraries. In fact strategic planning practices have become so wide-

---

Nancy M. Cline is Dean of Libraries at Pennsylvania State University, University Park, PA. Salvatore M. Meringolo is Assistant Dean and Head, Collections and Reference Services, University Libraries at Pennsylvania State University, University Park, PA.

201

spread that many managers are left with the distinct impression that the "whole of life" is indeed "spent thinking about how to find the right course of action to follow." The image that is frequently portrayed of the long hours devoted to planning is captured in the words of the senior manager offering some sage advice to the young, aspiring upstart, "Remember, some problems weren't meant to be solved . . . just worked on."

Ida Vincent in her article, "Strategic Planning and Libraries: Does the Model Fit?" raises some serious concerns about the application of strategic planning in libraries.[2] She argues that a mismatch occurs between the prevailing "normative model" of strategic planning and the needs of libraries, "partly as a result of certain structural characteristics of libraries, in particular their status as small and relatively powerless units in larger organizations . . ."[3] Six cases are examined from which the author further concludes that the "normative model" of strategic planning is deficient because it:

1. Assumes a sufficiently stable environment in which chosen objectives will remain viable;
2. Assumes that the organization will have excess resources to devote to strategic initiatives;
3. Requires a single, clearly articulated mission statement;
4. Presents the planning process as a linear, logical progression of steps.[4]

Ms. Vincent proposed that libraries seek strategic planning models which incorporate such characteristics as: incremental, bottom-up planning; the capability of dealing with dependence and uncertainty; acknowledgement of the significance of the individual and groups; and promotion of a planning mentality which permeates the organization, rather than limits itself to top management.[5] Indeed, strategic planning which is done in annual or triennial fits and starts can never hope to establish an organizational "planning mentality."

In 1979 Dan Schendel and Charles Hofer described a new management paradigm, strategic management, which would subsume and complete earlier work done on strategic planning. They defined strategic management as a "process that deals with the entrepreneurial work of the organization, with organizational renewal and growth, and more particularly, with developing and utilizing the strategy which is to guide the organization's operations."[6] The strategic management process consists of the following: (1) goal formulation — a process that is built upon the needs and relative power of the organization's various stakeholders; (2) environmental analysis — an investigation of external factors which the organization does not control and which may influence goals, strategy, and structure; (3) strategy formulation — the result of steps one and two and tempered by the strengths and weaknesses of the organization itself; (4) strategy evaluation — seeks answers to two basic questions — have existing strategies been any good? and will they be any good in the future?; (5) strategy implementation — begins after the selection and evaluation of proposed strategies; and (6) strategic control — focuses on whether strategies are implemented as planned and whether the results are those that are intended[7] (see Figure 1).

A critical aspect of strategic management relates to the strategy concept itself.[9] Different levels or types of strategy form a hierarchy as follows:

Enterprise strategy may be considered where the social conscience of an organization rests. Questions related to the organization's role in society are addressed here and impact all other strategy levels. A decision by a university to actively concern itself with the economic development of the private sector in its region through the formation of a research park may be considered an "enterprise strategy."

Corporate strategy asks the question, "What business should we be in?" Libraries may seek to answer whether they are passive repositories or active information providers. Universities may ponder their role as a continuing education provider for the adult learner.

Business strategy raises the question, "How should a firm compete in a given business, how should it position itself among its rivals in order to reach its goals, or how can it allocate its resources to achieve a competitive advantage over its rivals?" For the university or public library every department

FIGURE 1

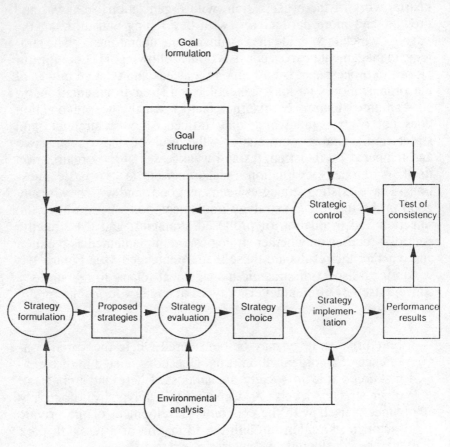

STRATEGIC MANAGEMENT PROCESS [8]

which competes for funds from the same funding agency should be considered "rivals" in the quest for a greater share of the resource pie.

Functional area strategies form the base of the strategy hierarchy and they are intended to integrate the various operational activities of the organization and to relate functional policies with changes in the functional area environment. Thus, a library's strategies to deliver and promote its instructional program will need to be coordinated with other public service programs which compete for resources.

The delineation of these various strategy levels is critical to strategic management because they recognize that "strategic planning" is not simply an exercise for the top management group. These various levels address the formulation, implementation, and coordination of strategy at every organizational level. Indeed, for the university library, most strategic work is at the "business" and "functional area" levels. Enterprise and corporate strategy will largely be in the purview of the university itself as it seeks to define its societal responsibilities as well as answers to the question, "What (new) businesses should it be in?" The directions set in these two strategy areas will guide the library's work in its strategic planning.

The introduction of strategic management can positively influence an organization's planning and will address some of the earlier mentioned criticisms of strategic planning by:

1. Helping managers at all levels plan for their areas of responsibility;
2. Providing information for making strategic decisions in a turbulent environment;
3. Serving as an organizational development tool to introduce orderly change;
4. Matching the allocation of resources with strategic directions;
5. Improving internal and external communications;
6. Providing an overall management framework or orientation for operating the organization.

That these strategic management components are widely reflected in the practice of management today confirms the notion that what Hofer and Schendel described was, and is indeed, a new management paradigm.

While strategic management provides an intellectually defensible construct for organizational planning, it should not be considered a linear planning prescription. The organization should rather seek to establish planning protocols which are most suitable for its particular type and size. The operational model which The Pennsylvania State University employs is most closely identified with the strategic planning techniques outlined by John M. Bryson for public and non-profit organizations.[10] His work deals primarily with a pragmatic approach to the formulation of strategy, and thus satisfies the first three strategic management conditions.

The emphasis according to Bryson should be on strategic thinking and acting, and not on strategic planning per se. Strategic planning is defined as a "disciplined effort to produce fundamental decisions and actions shaping the nature and direction of an organization's (or other entity's) activities within legal bounds."[11] The strategy formulation process which the author outlines consists of eight steps:

1. An agreement to engage in strategic planning and the framework which will be employed;
2. An identification of the organization's mandates, that is, what must it do to fulfill the basic requirements of its existence;
3. The development of the organization's mission and values— which together with its mandates—will complete its *raison d'etre*. A stakeholder analysis should be completed prior to the development of the mission in order to identify the claims that are placed on the organization by its various constituencies;
4. An external environmental assessment which seeks to identify the opportunities and threats from outside the organization;
5. An internal environmental assessment in order to identify the organization's own strengths and weaknesses;
6. The identification of strategic issues which result from the first five steps. Strategic issues deal with fundamental questions involving mandates, mission and values, product or service, constituents, finance, management, or organizational design;
7. The development of strategies to deal with the issues identified in the previous step;
8. A description of what the organization will look like in the future if strategies are implemented successfully.[12]

Beyond these eight steps, a strategically managed organization will also require that strategies be evaluated, implemented, and subject to control. It must be stressed that there are no singular approaches to strategic planning. There are indeed common characteristics as outlined in the strategic management process, but the application of the process should be determined by the organization itself.

THE PENN STATE
STRATEGIC PLANNING PROCESS

The guiding principle behind the implementation of strategic planning at Penn State was to raise the stature of the university among the nation's great universities. Penn State University is a comprehensive, multi-campus, research university, serving all regions of the Commonwealth of Pennsylvania as well as the nation and the world. In the University's *Strategic Planning Guide*, September 1984, President Bryce Jordan stated emphatically that an important goal of strategic planning was to create a clearer sense of direction for the University, in order to establish Penn State ever more firmly among the leading public universities of the nation.[13]

Five years later, in July 1989, a memo from William C. Richardson, Executive Vice President and Provost to University administrators, reaffirmed this point: "Strategic planning has provided the opportunity to create a vision for Penn State and to make policy choices consistent with that vision. Since 1983, the guiding principle for the University has been to enhance our position among the major internationally recognized public research universities." The University's mission statement that has evolved recognizes the mandates of multiple commitments to quality education for all students, the development of broad research programs, and the fulfillment of a variety of public services.

What happened in the intervening years, from 1983 to 1989, is of significant importance. Strategic planning was intended to enable the University to make decisions in a timely manner, to build upon existing strengths, and to provide the institution the ability to handle the changing forces affecting higher education.

The groundwork began in 1983 when Dr. Bryce Jordan, then newly appointed President of the University, initiated a program of strategic planning. His overarching goal was to take a great university and make it greater; to propel Penn State to a position among the premier public universities of the nation. The President appointed a University Planning Advisory Committee, to work in close cooperation with the Office of Planning and Analysis, providing a combination of faculty, administrator, and staff participation. Task forces conducted many initial assessments to develop a base of information reflecting strengths, weaknesses, opportunities and liabilities.

In the fall of 1984, many, if not most, participants in the process were skeptical. Most had been through previous episodes of "planning" and were keenly aware that many previous "plans" had been only partially implemented. The impact of this new "strategic" planning was not well understood, but this was a new President, with a bold vision, and it was obvious that the University was once again involved in planning. Essentially, the first phase was characterized by top-down guidance and plans were produced by the many academic and administrative units. Strategic planning at Penn State was organized around five aggregate planning units and twenty individual strategic planning units. The individual planning units included both academic and administrative organizational entities: Colleges, such as Agriculture, Arts and Architecture, Engineering, Earth and Mineral Sciences; the University Libraries; the Office of International Programs; Student Services; Finance and Operations, to name several such units.

The University Planning Advisory Committee had responsibility for guiding the development of the strategic planning program. As the Committee moved forward with its charge to review each of the plans and to criticize them, there was increased sensitivity among the deans and other administrators. These individuals were not accustomed to having their initiatives exposed in so broad a context and to subjecting their plans to committee review, especially by a group of individuals who might lack an appreciation for the specific details of a particular academic or administrative unit.

Nor was it easy to move so large and diverse a university to thinking in terms of selective enhancement of identified programs. Priorities had to be established among programs which were valued differently by different constituencies. In one sense, all parts of the University began to recognize that they were competing for enhancement status and funds, whether within a single unit or within the larger context. It became important to compare and evaluate using new methods. The concept of "environmental assessment," scanning for political, economic, societal, legislative/governmental impacts took on increased importance for all units.

The University Planning Advisory Committee read and evaluated all the plans and provided criticism. Careful consideration was made of the goals, specific objectives, alternative strategies, and the process and a written assessment was formulated. The Executive Vice President and Provost then reviewed the assessment and provided specific feedback to each unit. In many cases, in the early phases of the process, units were asked to provide better comparative data for the assessment of their programs' quality, depth, or breadth. Units were also reminded that strategic planning was regarded as an open process and that faculty and staff who participate in shaping and creating strategy are more likely to be enthusiastic about its implementation.

In the summer of 1985, the Provost carried out extensive consultation with the deans, vice presidents, and other administrators, providing guidance, reconciling major areas of oversight, and redirecting some initiatives. Each unit participating in the development of a strategic plan received written comments from the Provost. It was clear that an iterative process was underway.

In Fall 1985, the second round of strategic planning documents was submitted for review. At this point, the University began the process of linking the planning documents with the "resource allocation" process. These documents formed the basis of the budget request process, and while it was clear that there were very few new dollars for allocation, the distribution would be targeted to defined priorities and to those units or programs which had been designated for enhancement.

After 1985, rather than a complete rewrite of its plan, each unit was required to submit an annual update, identifying new or changing issues, evaluating progress toward implementation of goals, and reporting on the previous year's budget strategy. Many units' updates reflected considerable reallocation of existing budget resources during this timeframe.

Throughout the process, several fundamental guiding principles remained strong:

- The commitment by the Office of the President and the University's executive officers to authorize and use strategic planning as an instrumental component of decision making.
- The linkage of planning goals to resource allocation decisions.
- The comprehensive, University-wide application of strategic planning — at all locations, in both academic and administrative support areas.
- The incorporation of, or continuation of, accepted structures or processes (e.g., the annual planning and budget hearings) into the strategic planning process.
- A balance between top-down direction and bottom-up development of ideas and goals.
- The need to address in a timely fashion strategic issues that transcend traditional academic and administrative organizational boundaries.
- The notion that planning, to remain viable, must be ongoing, subject to change, and constantly evolutionary.

During the years from 1984-89 the University experienced considerable change. Penn State initiated various administrative and academic reorganizations in these past years and it has successfully withstood the changes. Among these are: the merger of two colleges to create a College of Health and Human Development; the creation of a School of Communications on a par with the academic colleges, the realignment of Student Support Programs; the establishment of the Office of Computer and Information Systems merging academic computing, administrative computing, and telecommunications into one central office; merging the office of the Dean of the Graduate School and the Vice President for Research and Graduate Studies; establishment of a Biotechnology Institute. Furthermore, a majority of the dean positions turned over, bringing new academic leadership to the colleges, the University Libraries, and the School of Communication.

After several years, communication improved among units as it became clear that the President planned to continue the commitment to strategic planning. There was a growing recognition across the University, that while the University Libraries was contending for funding, it was increasingly seen as a partner and less as a competitive threat to other academic funding requests.

It was also apparent that the linkage of resource allocation decisions, i.e., budget dollars to the planning process, gave impetus to a fuller commitment to planning. The annual budget hearings were clearly tied to the planning documents submitted by each administrative unit.

By the end of the first five-year planning cycle, most units had evolved to a combination of top-down direction and bottom-up development of ideas and goals. Deans and major administrators set in place major directions for their respective units, but in many cases, individual departments and programs adopted a recurring planning process that provided strong input from those most closely involved with the delivery of instructional, research, and service programs. This was certainly the case within the University Libraries where the priorities and specific plans of departments provided a strong base of information from which to develop a plan for the larger organization.

It also became obvious that several overarching issues extended beyond the scope of the various individual unit plans. In some instances, these issues were addressed by special strategic planning task forces: Academic Computing, Telecommunications, the Status of Women, Undergraduate Education, to name a few. Steadily, the recommendations from these special studies are being considered and integrated within the University's overall plans.

In 1989, the University embarked upon a second phase of strategic planning. The plans which had been written in the mid-eighties served as a benchmark but did not reflect the vitality of the new units and the input of the new leadership. The Provost and Executive Vice President issued the charge to administrators, outlining the new timeframe, and seminars were conducted in the fall to start the new phase with a charge to produce drafts of new strategic plans by March 1990. A newly appointed University Planning Advisory Committee II met in April, with the Provost and staff from the Office of Planning and Analysis to start the next phase of reviewing plans and advising units. Again, this committee would provide general guidance to the process.

A successful program of strategic planning takes time and requires commitment. For Penn State, it has been a sound investment, providing the institution with the ability to cope with change. Some of the changes affecting the University could be anticipated whereas some seem to arise with little warning. With campuses located throughout the Commonwealth of Pennsylvania, economic conditions in one region could change quickly affecting the programs and services of several campuses. The closing of a major plant could, for example, result in an influx of older non-traditional students or a need for more continuing education programming. For a large, complex university to be responsive to change, yet to not yield to short-term conditions which could undermine its strengths, requires that the institution know and understand its own mission and goals.

Penn State's President, Bryce Jordan, has announced his retirement, effective August 1990. The University is currently searching for his successor. At the same time, the Executive Vice President and Provost, William C. Richardson, will be leaving to become President at Johns Hopkins University. With these two executives departing the University within months of one another, the institution will experience a major transition in its leadership and its administration. There is not a question of halting the strategic planning process nor of waiting until a new President sets new directions. The strategic planning program provides a foundation which augurs a smooth transition. Based on the understanding of the University's mission and goals, charting strategic directions which respect those priorities that have been developed through an iterative process, and maintaining links to the budget allocation process, the institution is positioned to continue its pursuit of excellence.

THE UNIVERSITY LIBRARIES' APPROACH
TO STRATEGIC PLANNING

Background

The University Libraries' approach to strategic planning has continually evolved since the first effort in 1983. The initial plans were largely the product of the Dean's Executive Council which consisted of the Dean of Libraries and three assistant Deans. Additional input was provided by a committee which conducted an environmental assessment as well as from selected librarians representing various library locations in the Penn State system. However, since the University's planning process requires annual updates to the strategic plans of the various University units, a more representative, well-defined process was needed. In 1987, six additional library administrators were drawn into the strategic planning process in order to better reflect the needs of the operating units in the plan. In the Fall of 1988, the newly appointed Dean of Libraries formalized the work of a central planning group by creating the University Libraries Planning Council.

The two key elements that have energized the planning process in the University Libraries have been:

1. The linkage of the annual resource plan or budget request to the strategic plan;
2. The requirement that every academic and administrative unit of the University engage in planning.

The linkage of the annual budget request is a powerful motivating factor behind the strategic planning effort. The University administration has repeatedly stated that it will not fund initiatives that are not linked and represented in the strategic plan. This requirement insures that the strategic plan will not be relegated to collecting dust on a shelf. It has also provided strong incentives to move planning to the operational units of the Libraries so that current and future resource needs are accurately reflected in the budget request. The preferred outcome of the unit planning is a goals and objectives document which is supportive of the Libraries' strategic goals and represents the resource needs of that unit.

With every area of the diverse University community actively engaged in strategic planning, a "planning mentality" has begun to emerge. The strategic planning documents, particularly those of the academic areas, have been most useful in assisting the Libraries assess the University's information needs and to redirect resources to areas that have been designated for enhancement. For example, within the recent strategic plans of the College of Liberal Arts, certain departments were designed for enhancement, i.e., French, Anthropology, Psychology, and Philosophy. The enhancements received by these departments included the allocation of new faculty positions. The Libraries responded to this "strategic" decision within the College by providing modest enhanced support for collections in these four disciplines.

Mission and Goals

As was indicated above, the process by which the University Libraries has developed its strategic plans continues to evolve. The centerpiece of the current strategic plan is a mission statement which attempts to convey the complexities of a large research library in this age of information:

> The University Libraries, guided by the mission of the University, must support teaching, research, and service at all University locations by providing access to knowledge and information, through the use of appropriate storage, access and communications technologies. In doing so, the Libraries develop and manage collections and provide the space and interpretative services to support their use, as well as assume leadership in providing access to other information resources. The Libraries facilitate information access by forging a link to university, regional, national, and international information networks through participation in cooperative efforts which promote the sharing of information and access to the world's knowledge. In order to maintain its effectiveness, the Libraries, through its faculty, advances research in librarianship, information science, and scholarly communication.[14]

The mission statement is further defined by six overarching strategic goals:

1. Provide a comprehensive range of information resources and services to the Penn State academic community and the public.
2. Provide access and delivery mechanisms for a full range of information resources in all media in a networked research environment.
3. Strengthen the Libraries' unique role by providing leadership

in the areas of scholarly communication and information management.

4. Strengthen the role of the Penn State Libraries in state, regional and national networks.
5. Play a leadership role in the development and implementation of programs which support University instruction and the information literacy needs of students.
6. Develop a coherent infrastructure for library/information management and planning.[15]

Since 1988, these goals have formed a framework for the Libraries' annual budget request in which every item in the request is prioritized and indexed to one or more of the strategic goals. Thus, for example, the Libraries' needs statement for resources to develop and manage its collections is linked to the first strategic goal.

Strategic evaluation and control is largely exercised through the budget process at two critical points. The first is the Libraries' own prioritization of its resource needs. The strategic planning process continually identifies new resource needs which are in the vicinity of 20-25% of the base budget. Past practice has made it clear that new University funding in excess of 5% of budget is highly unlikely. Thus, the strategic importance of every item in the budget request must be evaluated closely, particularly those that are not prioritized within the first 5%. The second hurdle occurs at the University level where the Libraries' significant budget needs compete against strong "needs statements" and strategic plans of other areas. The limits to enhanced funding opportunities provide strong incentives to develop alternative means of enhancement primarily through reallocating resources or developing external funding sources such as grants or private gifts.

The University Libraries' plan to develop networked access to subject databases provides a good example of a budget decision that leads to an evaluation and change in strategy. The initial strategy, which was linked to strategic goal number two and outlined in the Libraries 1989/90-91/92 Strategic Plan update, requested a considerable allocation for the purchase of a vendor's search software system, as well as appropriate hardware upgrades, and selected databases. The budget allocation which was received by the Libraries for the 1990 fiscal year did not contain funding for this initiative. Faced with two extreme positions of resubmitting the proposal with the next strategic plan or dropping it, the Libraries has chosen a middle course of action — to enhance and extend to other databases the search software used to search LIAS, Penn State's own public access catalog. While the development time for these enhancements will delay implementation for at least two years, the final product will present the user with familiar search protocols in addition to its being a much less costly solution.

Other strategic initiatives of the Libraries have received a more immediate response from the University. For example, as a result of the serious erosion of the Libraries' purchasing power in its acquisitions programs due to dollar devaluation and inflation, the University has agreed to a formula approach to maintain purchasing power in these accounts. Now in its second year, this program has insured that serial price increases and approval plan cost increases do not negatively impact the balance of the acquisitions budget.

New Strategy Formulation

The University and the Libraries are currently engaged in a comprehensive review of strategic plans for the 1991/92-1994/95 which will most likely involve a revision to the Libraries' mission and goals statements. The following diagram illustrates the process that is being employed by the Libraries to identify strategic issues in this round of planning (see Figure 2).

The University kicked off the current round of strategic planning with an all day Strategic Planning Seminar which was held in September 1989. The seminar was sponsored by the University's Office of Planning and Analysis and was attended by over 200 key planning individuals from the various academic and administrative areas of the University. John Bryson from the University of Minnesota's Hubert H. Humphrey Institute of Public Affairs was brought in to discuss the role of strategic planning and to outline his strategic planning model. One of the outcomes of an afternoon series of small group discussions was the identification of strategic issues which would help guide strategic planning over the next several years. The most prevalent issues that were identified by the groups

FIGURE 2

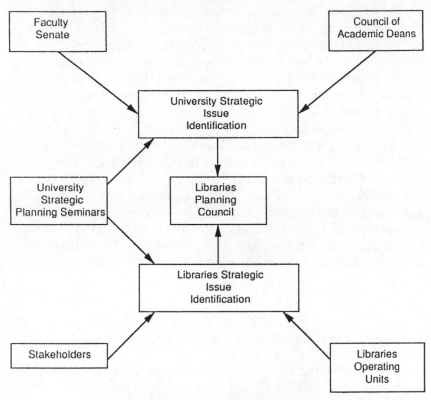

STRATEGIC ISSUE IDENTIFICATION

included: funding, diversity, technology and information management, university-industry ties, educational quality, international-
ism, institutional image, space and facilities, faculty quality, enrollment, and effective management. The Faculty Senate and the
Council of Academic Deans have also had the opportunity to comment on, and contribute to, the development of the University's list
of strategic issues. As the Libraries began its own deliberations,
these strategic issues formed a basis upon which to identify its own
strategic concerns.

In an attempt to further identify the strategic issues and environmental concerns which confront the Libraries, the Planning Council
solicited input from every department within the Libraries. Forms

were distributed and used to record this information. The Strategic Issue Workform asks each unit to identify the strategic issues, explain why it is an issue, indicate the consequences of not addressing the issue, and outline a possible action plan for addressing the issue. An environmental assessment worksheet was also distributed in order to gather feedback about opportunities, threats, strengths, and weaknesses that the Libraries must consider in its planning.

The Planning Council also scheduled meetings with a series of "stakeholders" in an attempt to gather additional input for its new strategic plan. Over twenty "stakeholders" who represent key constituencies for the Libraries, such as the College Deans, were asked to share information about their college's major strategic direction and whether there are new or strengthened areas which will require additional library support.

This input from the Libraries' units and from its external constituencies, as well as information carried forward from earlier strategic plans, forms the basis for the work on strategy formulation in the new strategic plan.

STRATEGIC PLANNING: DRAWBACKS AND BENEFITS

Strategic planning as it has been conducted at Penn State University has definite drawbacks that are nevertheless outweighed by its benefits. The "downside" of strategic planning includes the following:

1. It can raise expectation levels within the Libraries as well as among constituents. Identifying $3 million of additional resource needs and receiving only one fifth of that amount can create disillusionment with the process. Strategic planning by itself will not create additional funding sources.
2. Strategic planning is time consuming because it is ongoing and requires the attention of many individuals in the organization.
3. Strategic planning requires the participants to work in a number of different timeframes—generally from two to 5 years from the present. It can sometimes be difficult to attach resource needs to proposed strategic initiatives which are that far into the future.

The benefits that have been realized as a result of strategic planning include the following:

1. The broad implementation of a system of organized planning at the operational levels of the Libraries.
2. Bottom-up input into the planning process provides a vehicle for institutionalizing a participative management system. A major tangible benefit includes the more accurate representation of the total resource needs of the various Libraries' units. As a result, the Libraries has elevated the resource needs of the "core service" areas to a top strategic priority. New initiatives are therefore balanced against the needs for additional staff and equipment to augment current operations.
3. Internal organizational communications have been improved as planning documents are shared across departmental units.
4. A shared understanding of the multiple missions of the components of the University community is promoted; these various plans are of significant importance to the Libraries which must support their changing teaching, research and service needs.
5. The Libraries' ability to communicate its "story" to the other areas of the University community is enhanced as are the opportunities to form "political alliances" with various constituent groups.
6. Attention is focused on, to quote President George Bush, the "vision thing." Perhaps the more relevant question than, "What business are we in?" is "How can we do our business differently, or more effectively?"
7. Serves as a beacon around which an organizational consensus and commitment are built and it can help define an organization's values.

CONCLUSION

Without doubt, the strategic planning process can be strengthened and improved. A closer look at many of the written planning documents indicates there are areas where senior leadership might elicit a closer working relationship among units, require a greater degree of selectivity for areas of enhancement, or provide for stronger, closer correlation with prevailing political or economic conditions to which the University is subject. However, too much tightening in the context of an academic enterprise threatens to quench the spark that has characterized the commitment to date. If too heavy a hand is applied in editing, refining, controlling the planning documents or if the goals are too finely crafted by a central office and then handed down, there is a likelihood of resistance. Ownership must evolve and shared goals derive from collegiality.

The process does need additional means of evaluation. With so few new budget dollars to distribute, the viability of one's strategic plan cannot be tied solely to the success in the budget request cycle. To incorporate more discussion with the Provost of the merits of one's plans would be beneficial. Certain issues could be discussed in academic planning sessions so there is opportunity to explore different points of view and to perhaps devise collaborative solutions. This now occurs occasionally and is generally an informal process.

The investment made in strategic planning at The Pennsylvania State University appears to be well worth the effort at this juncture. Strategic planning has been concerned with establishing the major directions from which operational objectives are developed. These broad strategic directions for the Libraries have included case statements for space and facilities; core services which have been defined as bibliographic control and access, and reference and instructional services; collections; and new technology initiatives. While strategic planning has produced some significant resource gains for the Libraries, those strategic initiatives which have not yet been addressed with resource allocations are just as important. With each subsequent planning effort, the Libraries is challenged to reassess or find new approaches to addressing these issues.

Organizations must resist the tendency to overly formalize the process of strategic planning. Each planning effort at Penn State, and certainly within the University Libraries, has employed various techniques and approaches. The University has not dictated a prescribed approach and this lack of rigidity in the process has had a positive effect on the inventiveness of the various units. It is our hope that a strategically managed University Libraries will be the ongoing legacy of strategic planning at Penn State.

What has resulted at Penn State is an environment in which strategic planning is an ongoing and vital process, tied into the allocation of resources. It is a process which is a clearly designated priority of the administration, and it is as integral to the administration and management of the University as the annual budget cycle.

NOTES

1. Steiner, George A. *Strategic Planning: What Every Manager Must Know*. New York: The Free Press, 1979: p. 344.

2. Vincent, Ida "Strategic Planning and Libraries: Does the Model Fit? *Journal of Library Administration* 9 (March, 1988) pp. 35-47.

3. Vincent, p. 37.

4. Vincent, pp. 42-43.

5. Vincent, pp. 44-46.

6. Hofer, C. W. and Schendel, D. E. *Strategic Management: A New View of Business Policy and Planning*, Boston: Little, Brown, 1979: p. 11.

7. Hofer and Schendel, pp. 14-18.

8. Hofer and Schendel, p. 15.

9. Hofer and Schendel, pp. 12-13.

10. Bryson, John M. "A Strategic Planning Process for Public and Non-Profit Organizations," *Long Range Planning* 21 (January, 1988) pp. 73-81.

11. Bryson, p. 74.

12. Bryson, pp. 74-77.

13. Pennsylvania State University. *Strategic Planning Guide*, 1984.

14. Pennsylvania State University Libraries. *Strategic Planning Update*, 1988.

15. Ibid.